Choose

Choose

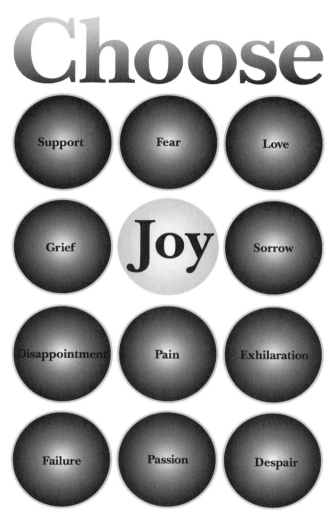

Support Fear Love

Grief **Joy** Sorrow

Disappointment Pain Exhilaration

Failure Passion Despair

By Francis W. Kelley and Geoffrey F. Spencer

With Supporting Testimonies

Herald Publishing House
Independence, Missouri

Table of Contents

Preface

In recent years there has been an increase in the development of religious literature designed to identify spiritual meaning encountered in everyday life. Each type of religious literature has its own style and vocabulary. In the Reorganized Church of Jesus Christ of Latter Day Saints with the coming of the Temple and the church's declared "peace mission," the need for a different kind of literature than has generally been produced has become more apparent.

Recognizing this need, Geoffrey F. Spencer and Francis W. Kelley, ministers of long tenure and broad experience, responded to the need to write in this field. Their present offering will enable some readers to tap the wellspring of the celebration of life in all its fullness and beauty.

As is true of other words in the Christian vocabulary, the common meaning of "joy" is used superficially, as is true when joy is equated with happiness. There is a large resource of experience to meet these needs as they come to our attention at the present time. This storehouse of experience is recorded in people's lives and more particularly is to be found in the testimonies of many practicing Christians, including those of our own faith, who have been able to identify the highly significant meanings in the ordinary experiences of life.

Geoff Spencer and Frank Kelley bring unique gifts and experience to this task. The former has long been identified with the educational mission of the church and has made major contributions in his native Australia and throughout his long tenure in the United States with the World Church. He is a wise, insightful, humble servant of the Lord, so well demonstrated during his tenure as member and president of the Council of Twelve Apostles.

Frank Kelley has served as a missionary in French Polynesia. He has given leadership as president and chief administrator of several major field jurisdictions of the church. He has been a scholar his entire life. His range of interests is very broad and much of his ministry has been devoted to teaching and education.

Each author is a warm, sensitive human being with whom I have had the joy of close association for many years. Their work will commend itself, but I commend it to you because of its genuine insightfulness and because, indeed, they are my brothers in Christ.

Duane E. Couey

Foreword

The recent disposition to understand congregations of the church as "Communities of Joy" has helped to focus attention on an often-neglected characteristic of the faith. Perhaps our tendency to equate the gospel with soberness has blurred our recognition that life in the Spirit is cause for celebration, has muted the element of praise in our worship, and interpreted true discipleship as a grim, unsmiling business. Perhaps the previous absence of any reference to joy (like "grace") in the Book of Mormon index reflects a historic disinclination to rank joy high on the priority of virtues. Nevertheless, a closer study of the text, as demonstrated first in *A Complete Concordance of the Book of Mormon* (Herald House, 1950) by Arthur E. Starks, discloses more than a hundred references to joy, including the powerful injunction that "men [along with the rest of us] are that they might have joy" (II Nephi 1:115). References to "joy," "joyous," and "joyful" exceed the 140 mark in the much more recent *A New Concordance to the Book of Mormon* (Herald House, 1995) compiled by Hale and Barbara Lee Collins.

If the reported pronouncement to the shepherds abiding in the fields is to be believed, the coming of Christ brought "good tidings of great joy, which shall be to all people" (Luke 2:10). Given this understanding it is difficult to take issue with Maltbie Babcock's charge: "The Christian life that is joyless is a discredit to God and a disgrace to itself." The spectacular preacher of an earlier religious revival, W. A. ("Billy") Sunday insisted, "If you have no joy in your religion, there's a leak in your Christianity somewhere."

In this brief study we have endeavored to describe some of the circumstances and conditions in which we may experience the joy of the gospel. Some of these circumstances will not be happy or pleasurable conditions—indeed, they may be attended by pain, sorrow, and distress. Nevertheless, it is our thesis that joy is a basic orientation, an attitude, that illuminates and undergirds all the varied experiences of life, transcending and reshaping even the most grievous or threatening events that will confront most of us in the course of a lifetime.

We have each written an introductory statement on the nature of joy, which is followed by a series of chapters discussing the presence and power of joy in various situations or experiences. Admittedly the choice is limited; it is not possible to encompass the entire range of circumstances in which people have encountered joy. We hope not only to reflect on those dimensions of joy we have thought it appropriate to write about, but also to prompt your acknowledgment and celebration of other elements of experience that have brought you personal delight.

Since this project first began to occupy our attention, we have become more aware of something that we should, of course, have already known: the profound impact of joy in the lives of so many Saints. Joy has served as a sustaining and transforming force in virtually every conceivable circumstance. For this reason, in each chapter we have invited others to share testimonies of the ways they have come to know joy. To these friends and fellow Saints we extend our deep appreciation. Their testimonies have been a source of inspiration to us, as we trust they will be to you also.

We have concluded the study with chapters written by each of us in which we indulged ourselves in reflecting on one particular way we have uniquely found "exceeding great joy." We invite you to do likewise—to identify and give thanks for some particular avenue by which joy has impacted and enriched your life. Further, share your testimony. It is our conviction that the witness of the gospel and the vibrancy of our congregations is multiplied by the extent to which we "share the joy."

It is our hope that the explorations and testimonies shared in this book will supplement and confirm your own experiences of joy as one of the surest and most precious gifts shared in the congregations of the Saints.

Frank Kelley and Geoff Spencer

Chapter 1

Why  ?

Surprised by Joy (with Apologies to William Wordsworth)
By Frank Kelley

M. Scott Peck[1] begins his perceptive observations of human experience with the simple declaration: "Life is difficult." This is not necessarily a cry of desperation. It may well be a truly positive appraisal of our situation. Surely we know, if we are alert to what is going on, and if we have lived more than a very few years, that often those things that are not easily done, understood, or solved are ultimately the sources of our greatest feelings of accomplishment, personal satisfaction, meaning, and—yes, joy!

The hot, humid summers of my boyhood were often punctuated by cool suppers, designed to make the cooking and eating thereof simple and pleasant. One of my very favorite menus included cold Vienna sausages. Eschewed by today's high priests of nutrition, they were to me in those long gone days, fine fare. One July evening, in my omniscient adolescence, my father asked me if I *knew* what was in Vienna sausages. I read the label on the can. Aside from a number of bizarre organic elements best unmentioned (cheeks, lips, and so forth) a key ingredient was "animal byproducts"—evidently judged by the processors to be truly unmentionable.

Through that experience, I came to form the Vienna Sausage Principle: *Life's most meaningful and significant components, experienced as an infinite variety of insight and experience, are most often byproducts.*

One does not leave the house in the morning with "joy" on the

11

shopping list, any more than one can deliberately choose to grieve or be puzzled. Like other states of mind or experiences, joy is a byproduct. It occurs as a result of, or coincidentally with, other perhaps unrelated pursuits, occurrences, and relationships that, like these, may result from the activities or circumstances of the day. It is unique and often confused with lesser, more fleeting aspects of living. A quick perusal of popular dictionaries shows this to be the case. Here are two common definitions of "joy" that really deplete its true significance:

- **A very glad feeling, great pleasure, delight.**[2]

- **A condition or feeling of great pleasure or manifestation of such feeling: a source or object of pleasure or satisfaction.**[3]

If, as people of faith, we believe that real joy is defined for us in Holy Writ, we are faced with an interesting, complicated, but informative task. Old Testament Hebrew contains at least four different words translated as "joy," which appear most often to be communal or social expressions more than individual or private qualities. These expressions come in the form of praise, laughter, glad shouting—the articulation of worshiping and/or feasting communities—in response to the presence and blessings of God.

New Testament Greek gives us three groups of words that express the concept of joy. As in the Old Testament, joy is perceived as loud vocalizing in worship, group expressions in religious celebration, as well as a more individual experience or feeling. The view of joy unique to the New Testament is that it is seen as a result of the movement of the Holy Spirit and is not dependent on circumstances (a factor we hope will be treated at length and from many perspectives in this volume).

Our own Restoration scriptures reiterate the nature of joy as the result—by-product if you please—of the action of God in the lives of his children. Luke is clear that the "great joy" (Luke 2:10 IV) that will bless all people is the result of the coming of the Lord Jesus. Joy is listed as a "fruit of the Spirit" (Galatians 5:2). Latter Day revelation states clearly that joy is the consequence of the union of "spirit and element" (Doctrine and Covenants 90:5e). Lehi, in a singular statement both powerful and provocative, tells us that we are, that we might have joy—with joy defined as the ultimate reason for being, and the "fall" as the means by which all this might come to pass (See II Nephi 1:115ff).

The definition of joy is therefore neither simple nor without profound significance. We will attempt, in this work, to be careful to not equate it with mere happiness or feelings of pleasure and satisfaction. Our thesis is that joy is indeed a result of the Lord's grace, appearing to encourage, strengthen, and delight us in and through the wonderful mystery and variety of life's experience.

The Eternal Spring
By Geoff Spencer

Samuel Dickey Gordon put it this way: "Joy is distinctly a Christian word and a Christian thing. It is the reverse of happiness. Happiness is the result of what happens of an agreeable sort. Joy has its springs deep down inside. And that spring never runs dry, no matter what happens."

I do not know what was in the minds of the framers of the Bill of Rights as part of the U.S. Constitution (1791) in affirming one's right, among others, to the "pursuit of happiness." But the way it has frequently been interpreted and widely sought after has produced a two-edged sword. To the extent it has been equated with contentment, prominence, and freedom from stress, pain, frustration, or grief, it has been an elusive pursuit.

Happiness is assuredly a fragile experience. Most of us may indeed know times of happiness, but the mood tends to be fleeting and carries no lasting impact. And there are those who, to their enduring bitterness and sense of having been robbed of something precious, will claim never to have known happiness. As suggested by Samuel Dickey Gordon, happiness depends on favorable circumstances, such as to yield a surfeit of contentment or pleasure. Yet life rarely proceeds on a sustained measure of such high enjoyment, and even if it does, it seems to find happiness increasingly demanding and, for that very reason, increasingly elusive.

Our lives essentially consist of a wide spectrum of experiences. Some will yield pleasure, satisfaction, enjoyment, success, contentment, or laughter. Others will bring sorrow, pain, disappointment, failure, loss, or grief in their wake. Unless there is some element in our faith that accepts the first without unduly assuming their constancy, and is able to deal with the second without being permanently disabled, we shall find ourselves riding a roller-coaster, always grieving for the good times, but fearing the imminence of the "downers."

I recall one valued friend and associate who invariably was carried along on such a roller coaster. From a distance of about fifty feet each time I met him I could tell whether the next two or three hours would need to be given over to pastoral support and encouragement in an effort to lift him from the gloom of despondency into which he had fallen. I am reminded of the cynical attitude offered when all is not well:" "Cheer up, things could be worse. So I cheered up, and sure enough things did get worse."

Joy does not require us to gloss over or ignore the "trials and tribulations." There will be times for most, if not for all of us, when we will find ourselves pressed just to "survive in the wildness," to adopt a picturesque phrase coined by Stephen Covey.[4] Rather, joy equips us to confront these wilderness times with courage and honesty. In this respect, though we may "choose joy," as the title of this book suggests, we will most likely experience it as a gift—the by-product of a trust in and a commitment to the one we confess as the Christ. Like most gifts, it may come unbidden, as it were, even at times in the most unlikely of circumstances. We will be "surprised by joy," to mirror the poet William Wordsworth's conviction.

This is not to suggest that the achievement of joy is easy, or that its preservation under adverse circumstances follows without struggle. Like grace, joy may be free, but it is never cheap. There are times when joy will be sorely tested, as any gift may be. However, this should come as no surprise. Jesus sought to give his disciples a forewarning: "In the world ye shall have tribulation: but be of good cheer; I have overcome the world" (John 16:33).

There may well be experiences along the way, quite acceptable in themselves, that we might casually describe as joyful. Yet in many cases these experiences just do not have the depth to be sustained, but are fleeting, leaving no rich satisfaction in their wake. Often such experiences that masquerade as joyful will bequeath us a sense of paradise lost and an accompanying feeling of regret. We will find ourselves beset by a yearning to recover something that appeared to be so pleasing. The dead hand of nostalgia will prompt us to say, "If only…" or "Why did it have to end?" Of such times Eugene Field wrote:

> **All human joys are swift of wing,**
> **For heaven doth so allot it:**
> **That when you get an easy thing,**
> **You find you haven't got it.**[5]

It has always seemed a tragedy to me when from time to time I encounter people who are permanently discontented, even scarred, by the hopeless longing for some past time when life, as they remember it, was pleasing and joyful. One may long to duplicate the excitement of a winning touchdown, the pride of a full head of hair, the appeal of courting days, the zest and challenge of upward mobility. Such a futile longing for past "joys" appears to sour present experience, so that nothing ever seems quite to measure up to memory's regret.

Finally, to affirm that joy is a choice is not to say it is chosen out of thin air, as one might choose a preferred item from a menu. The gift is often born and cultivated in the crucible of trial, pain, or loss, and it matures as we address the whole range of human experiences that come our way with a profound trust in God. Nor is it immune to being tested. Nevertheless, if joy is indeed the fruit of the Spirit, then that Spirit is an "abiding comforter."

The reader may be tempted to think this is a facile or superficial claim. "It's one thing to speak about joy like that," you might say, "but it doesn't pan out that way in real life." All we can say is that we have found that abiding strength present in our own lives. When, in January 1998, our daughter and son-in-law lost their second child at the age of three weeks, both they and we found the resources to cope with a potentially crippling event in a way that passed understanding. In no way is this a solitary or unique experience. We have been amazed by the number of friends and fellow members of the church whose experience has differed from ours only in the specific circumstances. Indeed, it is difficult to perceive how we could live in the world with any sense of undeterred purpose and celebration were it not for the fact that we have been claimed by joy.

Notes

1. M. Scott Peck, *The Road Less Traveled* (New York: Touchstone, Simon & Schuster, 1978), 18.
2. *Webster's New World Dictionary* (New York: World), 791.
3. *American Heritage Dictionary*, Third Edition (Boston: Houghton Mifflin Co., 1992), 691.
4. Stephen R. Covey, *The 7 Habits of Highly Effective Families* (New York: Golden Books, 1997), 75.
5. Eugene Field, "Ways of Life."

Chapter 2

The Joy of Creativity

The Irrevocable Gift
By Geoff Spencer

For the gracious gifts of God and his calling are irrevocable.
—Romans 11:29 NEB

It is difficult to imagine how life would be without the potential to create, invested in every single human being. Our lives in community may often appear bewilderingly complex, the variety of human beingness just too wide to be grasped. The differences exhibited may give rise to every conceivable kind of problem, to be the root cause of a divisiveness that often impacts us with uncertainty, peril, and tragedy. Yet it is even more difficult to imagine the alternative: every human being a mirror image of every other individual. Under these conditions it would be difficult to think how we could use the term "individual" in any meaningful sense.

The differences in interests, skills, and abilities that characterize our human condition become evident very early in life. The differences defy any ready-made explanation. Although there are instances when children will exhibit a marked similarity to their parents in the matter of "giftedness," they are far outnumbered by the cases where there is a notable variation between the generations. Parents may often regret, or even grieve the fact that their children do not replicate or "carry on" their own strengths and abilities, but the distribution of gifts ranges free and unrestricted.

My own "profile" of abilities—and disabilities—showed up early in elementary school. Verbal skills came readily, while number skills—math, algebra, geometry—were a puzzle to me and a trial to my parents and teachers. Time had no apparent effect on the situation. I recall how vividly this was demonstrated when, as a member of a psychology class at Sydney University, I performed a battery of tests we would be expected to be utilizing as school counselors. Within one week I scored the highest in the class of eighty-five students in a test of clerical speed and accuracy, yet next to lowest in a test of mechanical skill and numbers comprehension. It was a source of amusement among my fellow students for some time.

It does not appear that wishing to change this order of things, or applying oneself diligently, makes any significant difference. While practice and experience may have some effect—after all I do manage to balance my checking account with reasonable success—the basic pattern is essentially established. People who graduated from the university with a bachelor's degree and were "bonded" to teach in the New South Wales Department of Education were required to earn a postgraduate diploma in education before being let loose on the children of the state. They were expected to choose, in addition to their education courses, a course in art or music as a release from the otherwise (allegedly) demanding schedule. Because my parents had both been more than adequate oil and watercolor painters, and my uncle, a nationally known artist, was art professor at the college, I decided to explore what to that point had been my hidden artistic talents. It was but a short time before my uncle suggested, very tactfully, that I might like to switch to music.

The expression of our talents and abilities brings with it the joy of creating—of producing, *ex nihilo*, as it were, something that is uniquely the product of our giftedness. I recall the satisfaction that accompanied the production of hymn texts for inclusion in *Hymns of the Saints* (Herald House, 1981) and for other settings. I expect that the same sense of joy is experienced by my wife in the creation of something quite beyond my skills—a garden. And the same joy must accompany a work of art or literature, a smoothly functioning engine, a finely tuned athletic skill, or the competent performance of any trade or professional calling in which years of training have been invested. How grateful we can be for the many faces of giftedness!

It is no accident that we commonly refer to the practice of our abilities as fulfilling a "calling." To give expression to our skills is at once a joy and a responsibility. A significant statement in the modern scriptures of the RLDS Church underscores the obligation that goes along with the power of creativity. Everyone thus empowered "should be anxiously engaged in a good cause, and do many things of their own free will, and bring to pass much righteousness; for the power is in them, wherein they are agents unto themselves" (Doctrine and Covenants 58:6d).

Further, while we will take pleasure and satisfaction in the expression of those skills, it is significant that we commonly refer to them as *gifts*. This is a confession that while we must take responsibility for developing or refining those skills, they come essentially as an endowment, a gift from outside ourselves. It is difficult to believe that we find a lasting joy either when we pride ourselves on possessing the skill or when we assume it is a private possession.

It is universally true that the possession of any particular skill constitutes a two-edged sword. I remember to this day with profound regret, the occasion when I joined my father in a discussion with a family that had only recently begun attending church again after a considerable absence. They were discussing some issues that the family had experienced difficulty in accepting. With full (eighteen-year-old) confidence in my powers of debate, I launched into the "contest." Returning home after church services that day I said to my father, with some prideful satisfaction, "Well, I think I won that argument." To this he replied, "Yes, you may have won an argument, but you lost a family." And so it turned out to be. The regret is only exacerbated by the fact that I now believe as the family did in registering their problem.

It is a joy to express our unique gifts of skill in creativity. It is well to remember from whence the freedom of creativity and the gifts come: "For every good endowment that we possess and every complete gift that we have received must come from above, from the Father of all lights, with whom there is never the slightest variation or shadow of inconsistency (James 1:19, Phillips).

In Gratitude for Her Gift
By Winifred Sarre

Few people in the life of the church have so delighted and in-spired others through a gift of singing as has Winifred Sarre of Adelaide, South Australia. Here she recalls the development and expression of that gift:

I have always loved to sing. At family sing-songs, campfires, and church services, singing was to me as natural as speaking. Some songs may have been nostalgic, sentimental, or even sad, but the singing of them was always a joy to me.

At seventeen years of age, full of confidence, I went to the Conservatorium of Music to study. I was taken aback when the rather fearsome teacher told me: "You have a beautiful voice, but you don't know how to sing." Thus began many months of breathing exercises, scales, vocal technique training, language, and repertoire study. For a while, what had been a source of joy seemed to become a source of stress. What had come naturally before now required concentration and thought. I felt like the caterpillar who, when asked how he could manage all those legs, suddenly found himself unable to do so. I became fearful, unable to do all that I was asked, sure I was never going to measure up.

I approached my first important concert with apprehension. Waiting for my entry, I felt I had forgotten all the techniques I had learned. Would I perform adequately? Could I think about interpretation when I was gripped by fear, almost terror? Would I manage to raise my voice at all? The moment came. I began. The voice soared—better, richer, higher. There was a rush of emotion, exhilaration, a prickling of the skin. The joy that flooded my being seemed to be in direct proportion not only to the tedious training I had undergone, but also to the fear that had preceded the performance. It was a joy greater than any I had experienced before.

Over subsequent years performances have come and gone, some better than others, some quite disappointing. But I have found that the greater the preparation, and even the greater the apprehension, the greater the joy. To create beauty of sound, to imbue it with the meaning of the words, to receive silent waves of response from the audience, all of these have fed the soul. It is, and has been, a joy for which I will always be grateful.

The Universal Bequest
By Frank Kelley

All ordinary expressions may be explained causally, but creative expression which is the absolute contrary of ordinary expression, will be forever hidden from our human knowledge.[1]

Parents always marvel at the creative powers of their offspring. Who has not been to a vacation Bible school, children's camp, or like gathering and not seen the outpouring of "crafts," artwork, and like memorabilia spread out for display at the close of these things? Surrounded by admiring throngs, the objects woven, painted, fired, carved, and/or dusted with glitter are lovingly gathered and carried home to some place of honor in the household. I grew up in such a milieu.

An older brother, off to war, had created a large sign for his bedroom door, advertising himself as an architect (which he did, in fact, later become). The room—and door—was as close as we came in Topeka to possessing our own Dome of the Rock and Holy of Holies. As I recall, it was long after the Allied victories that the sign finally came down, and I occupied the sanctuary hallowed by the habitation of both older siblings. The earlier, a musician in training, had left no tangible clue save faded snapshots of himself and George Hug resplendent in band uniform.

I grew up faced, as well, with my earliest attempt at artistic expression. On the wall in the corner where Mother did much of her sewing, hung a dingy orange plaster-cast—the imprint of a very small hand. Mildred Goodfellow had helped us children produce these in Sunday school. My name and the date sometime in

1940 or 1941—was scratched in the margin. My mother would not part with that artifact of an earlier, seemingly simpler age. I had made that thing, it represented me, and I was her own.

Much research into our nature as human creatures has been done in recent years. We know much more about ourselves now than at any former time. Much of what we know is incomprehensible. Jim Thornton, writing on recent brain explorations, states that "the minimum number of possible thought patterns is the numeral 1 followed by 6 1/2 miles of typed out zeros."[2]

Ken Simonton , Ph.D. and editor of the *Journal of Creative Behavior,* compared recognized creative people who have "burned out" with those who were still active and productive in their respective fields. His results showed that those still on the creating edge were individuals who *constantly exposed themselves to new knowledge or techniques.*

A Dutch psychologist, intrigued by all this, wondered about the differences between chess masters and chess grand masters. Tests were administered that showed that the IQs, spatial perceptions, etc., were comparable. Finally, he determined that the sole detectable difference between the two classes of chess experts was *the love of the game.* Evidently passion, too, is a key to creative process.

One of the key elements of our Judeo-Christian heritage that has enriched all of Western culture is the tenet that human beings are of inestimable worth. The foundation of such a view is found in Genesis 1, where we find humankind is to be made in the image and likeness of God. It is a source of wonder and delight to me that the very first attribute scripture has to reveal of this God in whose image and likeness we are made is that of *creator.* If the miniscule bits of understanding we have about ourselves are joined to that scrap we discern of the nature of Deity, we are confronted, I believe, with at least the following possibilities:

1. Created in the likeness of God, we are blessed with freedom and responsibility.
2. To the extent we attempt to truly mirror that divine nature, we too shall seek to be creative in the exercise of that freedom and responsibility, seeing creativity as a very real aspect of our own human stewardship.

3. We are summoned to participate in a world of moral confusion, ethical ambiguity, and competing value systems. The Lord is not to be found in this age simply repeating the same old things over and over. Latter-day inspiration consistently emphasizes that God does indeed make all things new, that we are called into a new and everlasting covenant relationship, and that the great and marvelous work is about to come forth. Again, the fundamental divine attribute of creativity is illuminated and underscored as God constantly uses new knowledge or techniques.
4. As the Creator loved what he has made, so we are called to respect and serve with *passion,* exhibiting in our lives the difference between "masters" and "grand masters" of the art of living fully.

In sum, creativity is not just found in the products of craft classes and the "making of things." It is not a gift or talent found only in certain rare individuals. It is more than an exercise in self-expression. It is a fundamental attribute of the divine nature, seeds of which are implanted in all of humankind, the development of which we are called to cultivate as we respond to the possibility of growing in God's likeness.

Long, long ago I ceased to fashion plaster casts of my little hand. I am sure, however, that still anything I choose to make, execute, speak, write, or fashion will positively identify me as its source. My hope is that I will learn the lessons of life well enough that whatever I create will rather bear witness to God as author and finisher of the work.

> **Men should be anxiously engaged in a good cause, And do many things of their own free will, and bring to pass much righteousness; for the power is in them, wherein they are agents unto themselves.—Doctrine and Covenants 58:6d**

And again, in a more contemporary setting, but in an equally joyful affirmation:

> **Be faithful to the spirit of the Restoration, mindful that it is a spirit of adventure, openness, and searching.... Laugh and play and sing, embodying the hope and freedom of the gospel.... Stand firm in the name of the One you proclaim and create**

**diverse communities of believers and seekers, rejoicing in the
continuing fulfillment of the call to this people...**[3]

Notes

1. Carl Jung, "Psychology and Poetry," June 1930, quoted in *Great Quotations*, ed. George Selds (Simon & Schuster, 1968), 240.
2. Jim Thornton, in *USA Weekend* (January 3, 1999).
3. W. Grant McMurray, "Words of Counsel" (April 1996).

Chapter 3

 **in Repentance**

Learning the Steps of the Dance
By Frank Kelley

"What is man…?" Seeking so very long ago, David asked, what is for humankind, that ultimate question (see Psalm 8:4). Every reflective person in every age has raised, in his or her own context, that very query. We are uniquely positioned, among all creatures, to wonder about such things. Norbert Schedler describes our circumstances thus:

Man is unique in that he stands out (meaning of "ex-ist") of what he is, and is able, therefore, to question the meaning of his being.[1]

Another agonized biblical thinker, Job, expressed his concern and bewilderment in terms with which most of us can relate:

A mortal, born of a woman,
Few of days and full of trouble,
Comes up like a flower and withers,
Flees like a shadow and does not last.—Job 14:1 NRSV

More recent scripture describes Moses raising this same issue with his God, asking: "Tell me, I pray thee, why these things are so…" (Doctrine and Covenants 22:20).

Furthermore, in the story of our own denomination, we feel that simply raising questions is not the key to deep relationship with the Almighty (see Doctrine and Covenants 9:3). This pursuit, this driven search for the reason for our being, and the answer to the question, "Who and what am I?" plagues our own age as well. R. S. Thomas, a Welsh poet, seeks his own solution, and is not specially pleased to find humanity here

**Shipwrecked upon an island
in a universe whose tides
are the winds.**[2]

Shedler helps our understanding of the issue by adding this perspective:

Historical situations vary; a man may be born a slave in a pagan society or a feudal lord or a proletarian. What does not vary is the necessity for him to exist in the world, to be at work there, to be there in the midst of other people, and to be mortal there.[3]

Being "mortal there" includes a fundamental hunger to know fundamental things. What is it that fuels this search for meaning and identity? Marjorie Hewitt Suchocki has likened our circumstances to a party:

We look around us, and if we dare to admit it, within us, it seems the dance has gone awry. Perhaps some invisible violinist is out of tune, or the drummer is deaf, giving an off-beat. Or perhaps we simply haven't learned the steps of the dance too well.[4]

Since the far distant past Christians have leaned on a tradition, supported by scriptural interpretation, institutional practice, and personal unease. This tradition has sought to explain our hunger for existential understanding by assuming that we are seriously and fatally flawed. The flaw is described as a defect, universally afflicting humanity. We are found culpable, individually and as a species, declared to be possessed of a nature in opposition to and rebellion against our Creator. This behavior, described as sin, is both inherited and individually enacted as willful conduct.

Organized religion—including our own tradition—has sought to prescribe remedies for this affliction. For many Christians these have taken the form of confessing and admitting to a regrettable nature and conduct, seeking and accepting the forgiveness of God as extended through the life, ministry, death, and resurrection of the Lord Jesus, and vowing to live a life of goodwill and works, as defined by scripture and church. In return, the living presence of the Holy Spirit as personal guide and companion is promised, as well as an afterlife of happiness and satisfaction.

This process of correctly "learning the steps of the dance," to use Suchocki's metaphor, is known as *repentance*. Repentance is customarily described as the experience of contrition and a probationary agenda following righteous judgment. Alternative perspectives are available. It is possible to view repentance from a point of view other than that of a compulsively sinning, defective, unworthy creature. Karl Menninger, for example, in his remarkable treatise on sin, writes that sin is, "at heart, a refusal of the love of others."[5]

The state of sin has traditionally been described as separation from God. This can be understood as temporary, a developmental state, one of transition—not always entirely or simply the result of willful human transgression. Repentance can be appreciated as the process of becoming what we are meant to be, the metamorphosis leading to true joy. Don Compier, a member of the faculty of the Church Divinity School of the Pacific (Berkeley, California) and an elder in the RLDS Church, puts it this way:

> **I would argue that joy derives from becoming what we are created and called to be by God…. It is a quality of being whole and having integrity. Fulfilling our purpose… that sense of inner confidence and positive acceptance and regard for life, that sense that one is on the right track and heading in the right direction.[6]**

For another RLDS author, L. Wayne Updike, repentance is "a conscious positive response to an ever-increasing revelation of God."[7] Paul Hessert agrees that repentance is a dynamic, writing that it is "the basic Christian approach to life, appropriate to every stage."[8] Kathryn Tanner reinforces this point of view in affirming that Christians "are required, that is, according to the original Greek sense of the term 'repentance' to turn around and rethink their Christian commitments."[9]

Repentance, as an experience and process of joy, is best summarized for me in the experience of a dear friend I'll call "Jake." I met Jake in an adult-level graduate education class. He was big, good-natured, and constantly smiling. Circumstances threw us together in a mutual project. One evening, over coffee and dessert, he mentioned his near-death experience. I learned that, at less than thirty years of age, he had suffered three open-heart surgeries and that on the last occasion he had sensed an out-of-body transition. I urged him to tell me about it, as I had read accounts of such happenings but had never spoken to a participant. "I can't tell you," he said. "There are no words to describe it. I didn't see a light at the end of a tunnel, nor was I approached by personages or deceased loved ones." At this point, Jake's countenance changed and he appeared almost luminous. "I know this much," he said with greater intensity, "we're here to learn, not to fix things or each other. *We are here to learn.* Understanding that has changed my life."

As I came to know and love Jake, I did not discover a creature twisted by sin and condemned by the demands of an eternal code of justice, looking forward to possible redemption in some heaven on "the other side." I found a man who mined each day with great expectations for the here and now, who understood clearly the admonition of Thich Nhat Hanh, who wrote:

> **If we cling to our ideas of hope in the** *future***, we might not notice the peace and joy that are available in the present moment. The well is within us. If we dig deeply in the present moment, the water will spring forth."[10] [Emphasis mine.]**

There is no question that we are imperfect. Christians know that the struggle to understand, to grasp the meaning of things—the tensions of dealing with imperfection—is called repentance. True repentance leads to growth; learning the steps of the dance, understanding we are in the process of asking those ultimate questions, and becoming what we are called and created to become, leading into authentic salvation. Macrina Wiederkehr describes the joy in it all:

> **We are saved every day. We are saved from our self-righteousness, our narrow minds, our own wills, our obstinate clinging. We are saved from our blindness. Our frailty fades into splendor. Our frailty need not cripple us, our glory need not be denied. Embraced and cherished as part of the process that we are, these qualities become God's greatest advantage in our lives.[11]**

Turning and Returning
By Laurie Gordon

I stand, face upturned, under rain-drenched redwood trees in the midst of a torrential downpour. I have fled the confined comfort of my discontented life and ventured out into the heart of this storm. The reasons I carry a heavy and hardened heart are not important for this telling. What is important is the turning about to reconnect with life. I have climbed but a short way. The trail in front of me has become a bubbling, garrulous cascade of run-off from a day and night of nonstop deluge. Tree branches drip fiercely, unburdening themselves of the accumulating weight. The forest calls me to participate in its verdant aliveness. Redwood-filtered rainwater streams down my face, warming from the heat of my skin as it runs, until it is as if I were crying all the unspent tears I have never been able to loose. Three words arise: cleansing, baptism, renewal. One feeling arises: joy. This is a moment of turning and returning. I leave behind separation and come home to God. I die to what has been and rise to what lies ahead.

I must admit to a gut-level resistance to the word "repentance," a sometimes violated concept that begs reconsideration. It has become layered with false, or at least misleading, inferences that distance us from its truer meanings. The movements of repentance allow us to participate in the turning from death to life that is the heart of the Christian message. The joy springing and turning from what separates to what reconnects is the transforming joy of resurrection. Yet, unfortunately, too often "repentance" conjures an image of groveling rather than conveying intimations of joy. God is made out to be a stern judge of our misactions rather than the "Ground of Love" inviting a return to wholeness. That repentance serves a shame-based ideology is evident from the ways we joke about it. When I was asked, innocently, by this book's authors, to write a short testimony on the "joy of repentance" my first reaction was to worriedly question what it was about my life that made them think I had needed to repent!

Let me be careful here. It's not that I have never begged God's forgiveness in a panic-stricken fit of guilt for some word or action for which I felt unrelenting shame and self-recrimination. But the aftermath of such hotpoint acts of contrition, whether the breach between me and God is real or perceived, is often more relief than joy. In these "groveling" events I have been driven by my need to feel better about myself more than by a naked desire to reforge a severed relationship with the interconnected patterns of life and love that we call God. There are major turning points in life requiring deep changes in order to reorient the course of one's path into the future. My experience is that these redirections usually entail extended periods of transformative interaction before generating a lasting joy. Quick relief from the burden of guilt is a poor substitute for the deep and enduring joy that accompanies lifelong returning to God.

The Hebrew word from which the word "repent" originates means "to return." In the suffering of a people estranged from their homeland, Israel experienced the core meaning of repentance stamped with the heartbreak of exile and the joy of homecoming. I know something about being homesick, having suffered from it repeatedly in the course of my lifetime. Acute homesickness carries with it a pervasive, aching sense of disorientation and disconnection. Cut off from the places and people that I love, it is a wandering, displaced, "stranger in a strange land" yearning for reintegration and restored relationships. In one form or another, the homesickness of exile is the precursor to those events of turning and returning that continue to transform my life.

I first experienced the nauseating discontent of exile as a teenager when I left home, socially inept and painfully shy, to pursue a course of studies at a state university. I now recognize with the clarity of hindsight that the directions I was taking at that time were leading me away from my true self and my true place in God's patterns. Pursuing studies that did not match my personality in a place where I made few friends and was unrelentingly distanced from family caused months of anxious emotional turmoil and seemingly directionless struggle. The homesickness got worse for a while when I changed course and packed myself off to the church college (Graceland) I had previously stubbornly resisted. In Iowa I was stranded for months at a time two thousand miles from my California home. But instead of separation I was graced with a community that offered me love, the pursuit of interests closer to my heart, and a nascent relationship with God as Mystery. The initial actions leading to this critical turning point for my life were not shameful, but they had charted the wrong course for my future. My choices needed redirecting, a turning about that was enormously difficult, but that led, inevitably, to homecoming.

Because I know homesickness so well, I also know something about the poignant, explosive joy of homecoming after a long sojourn in the wasteland. I will never forget the profound, indescribable sense of completeness I experienced when I walked off the airplane to the feet of ocean-kissed air whispering "home" into the arms of my waiting family. By the time of my physical return, I had already come home to myself, to life, and to God in more fundamental ways. I am not speaking of a giddy, passing relief to return to things as they once were. I am speaking of the renewal of connectedness in which I came home to the ground of love as a woman changed by the pain of separation. To this day, whenever I return from sojourns far afield, home is never the same, because I am never the same. This joy of turning and returning—that is, the joy of repentance—is the joy of reintegration following on the heels of disintegration; it is lasting and deep, encompassing suffering as well as the beauty of love's renewal.

As the years go by, I find myself occasionally feeling homesick even though I am physically in my own space and surrounded by the people I love. This used to confuse me until someone pointed out that I was homesick for my true home in the heart of God. In a way I experience the homesickness of exile daily, whenever the patterns of my life disconnect me from the intimacy of God's love. I repeatedly experience homecoming whenever I return to right relationships within an intertwined web of life permeated by God.

Repentance is an ongoing process that never ends. Each of us could relate a dozen simple testimonies about the many movements

of repentance. I have experienced turning from
- aching loneliness to silent solitude
- hostility to hospitality
- suspicion to trust
- indifference to compassion
- wasteful consumption to sacrificial living
- apathy to enthusiasm
- intolerance to acceptance
- manic business to silent resting
- holding on to letting go
- fear to vulnerability
- destructive anger to constructive action
- boredom to awe.

In these many instances, repentance is a movement from bondage to freedom, from exile to homecoming, from death to life. Rather than a shame-based action, repentance is a transformative process, turning us step-by-step into the image of Christ that is in us. It is a daily (weekly, monthly, lifelong) turning and returning to God.

The opportunity for joy is embedded in every turning and returning. A few of those moments of joy are intense and recognizable, as in the story with which I opened this piece. Some moments of joy are bittersweet, impregnated with pain as much as with happiness. Many, many more moments of joy simply accumulate quietly. In repentance we reenact the mystery of dying and rising into newness that is the essence of the Christian way. Repentance anticipates resurrection.

Humankind Is No Lemon
By Geoff Spencer

Don't do this, and don't do that;
Repent, repent, repent.[12]

Many years ago, intrigued by the title, I purchased and read a book by John M. Krumm titled *The Art of Being a Sinner,* doubting that I had anything more to learn about the art. At one point the author describes the personal (though surely not unique) experience of buying a used car, only to discover in the course of time its many imperfections and breakdowns. Krumm persisted with the vehicle, despite its repeated failures, perhaps unwilling to face the fact he had made a sad mistake. The story continues:

A friend of mine passed eloquent but accurate judgment on the car when he said flatly, "Let's face it; you got a lemon!" He went on to say that nothing I could do to fix it would really be satisfactory because the car was, somehow, basically all wrong.... That is the judgment of many people—including some of the world's great religions—about human existence.[13]

Is it true that human existence is indeed inherently a lemon, constitutionally and irredeemably self-destructive? Paul cried out, in torment: "O wretched man that I am! Who shall deliver me from the body of this death?"(Romans 7:26 IV; 7:24 others). Is the correct answer "Nobody and nothing"? Are we merely tiny parts of the great universal lemon?

The Christian answer is at the same time discouraging and hopeful. We are indeed fatally flawed by a malady that appears to be universal. Moreover, we don't contract this disease by any conscious effort on our part; all we need to do is go with the flow, so to speak. In this respect the biblical witness likens us to sheep (see Isaiah 53:6).

At the same time, Christian faith declines to describe the disease, ultimately, as terminal. We can, by the gracious initiative of the One who presides over life and history, rise above the condition beseting us. We can, to use an image lifted up previously in this chapter, position ourselves to "learn the steps of the dance." The theological term for this process is *repentance*.

Admittedly, for many this is indeed a tiresome and painful process. If the concept embedded in the old camp song quoted above is true, then repentance is nothing more than a matter of giving up, doing without, ceasing to do something that has been pleasurable, sacrificing, forsaking. From this point of view, the title of this chapter is an oxymoron, emphatically self-contradictory. How can there be any shred of joy in such repenting? It would appear to be a grim and joyless process indeed, much like being condemned to a daily trip to the dentist for a root canal. Even Jesus appears to draw our attention away from the joy of celebration back to the hard demands of living in response to the gospel. When he encountered a woman who appeared to enjoy her praise, Jesus interrupted her, saying, in effect, "Enough of the praise, get on with the business of obedience" (see Luke 11:27–28/11:28–29 IV). I comfort myself by the suspicion that Jesus was making a humorous response to curb a woman's excess of enthusiasm.

On the other hand, it does appear that some people "enjoy" repentance, almost allowing themselves to be overcome by pride in confessing what great sinners they have been and how greatly their repentance is to be held in reverence, even envied. I have occasionally gained the impression that a kind of contest could be made of the matter: "I have been a more miserable sinner than you, so *my* repentance is greater than *your* repentance." There is an underlying hint that repentance is something to be admired, related to the magnitude of what one has given up, quit doing, gone without, denied.

If you will forgive my momentary descent into cynicism, I will still assert that there is an element in repentance that induces soberness. In general, and until recently, it was not fashionable to introduce the topic of sin, especially one's own, into polite conversation. It has even been of borderline acceptance to allow the practice of confession of faults into a religious setting, despite its established therapeutic value (see James 5:14–16). It is almost as if the subject touches too closely and painfully on our awareness of the human condition, so that it is safer to acknowledge "sin" in general, without getting too specific. Nevertheless, the English theologian Alan Richardson pinpoints this distressing situation, universally experienced, if not universally acknowledged:

It is...universal ... *in the sense that it is relevant to the predicament of* **every individual person coming into the world, as a creature who is (however dimly) aware of himself as in rebellion against the purpose for which he exists and as helpless to redeem his condition, a creature whose mortality mocks his longings for eternal fulfillment and creates in him that anxiety which he vaguely knows to be the symptom of his estrangement from his own true being and destiny.**[14]

And so, as an advertisement some years ago popularized the saying, "Where's the beef?" we might ask, "Where's the joy?"

A fundamental element of repentance, often overlooked, is lifted up in the Old Testament, particularly in the prophetic literature. Here repentance is understood as the imperative to restore and preserve the covenant with God, by whose terms we are to be more merciful and just toward each other, indeed to do justly and to love mercy (see Micah 6:6–8). The process went beyond individual sorrow and self-adjustment, but envisaged a redeemed humanity living in mutual support and affirmation. This perspective turns attention away from the grim business of giving up enjoyable things, sacrificing activities that yield satisfaction, and in otherwise taking all the enjoyment out of life. Rather, it holds out the promise of joy on a higher, more enduring level. At the same time it is a stance that releases us from self-absorption, either from the pride of achievement or the pain of sacrifice. Certainly it may involve the experience of being sorry for past ways of behaving, but, as Krumm observes: "The hopefulness of being sorry is that it is the basic condition of health."[15] It is as if somebody were to counsel us, "Do yourself a good turn—repent."

Finally, the human condition *is* redeemable, and in ways that far transcend the grimness of some understandings of repentance:

The human species evolved very slowly, with consciousness and *self-***consciousness emerging out of animal conditions dominated by instinct and motivated by an anxious self-protectiveness. That we must struggle to find reconciliation with God, self, and neigh-**

bor is not the result of some willful disobedience that destroyed a primeval paradisal state. It is rather the result of evolutionary developments that are not properly understood in legalistic or moralistic terms. Because of this shift, a rethinking of the cause and character of humanity's problem has occurred.[16]

We are not irredeemably reduced to a grim and joyless struggle that brings pain and renunciation at every step. Nor are we, individually or universally, of the constitution of a lemon. We are creatures who have taken the first steps necessary for health and find ourselves empowered, under God, to share in the emerging new humanity. This is occasion for great joy.

Notes

1. Norbert Schedler, *Philosophy of Religion* (New York: MacMillan Company, 1974), 121.
2. R. S. Thomas, *No Truce with the Furies* (Newcastle Upon Tyne, U.K.: Bloodaxe Books, 1995), 43.
3. Norbert Schedler, 135.
4. Marjorie Hewitt Suchocki, *God, Christ, Church: A Practical Guide to Process Theology* (New York: Crossroad, 1986), 22.
5. Karl Menninger, *Whatever Became of Sin?* (New York: Hawthorn Books, 1973), 19.
6. Don Compier, private correspondence in files of author.
7. L. Wayne Updike, *Whosoever Repenteth* (Independence, Missouri: Herald House, 1957), 15.
8. Paul Hessert, *Introduction to Christianity* (Englewood Cliffs, New Jersey: Prentice-Hall, Inc., 1958), 174.
9. Katherine Tanner, in Rebecca C. Chopp and Mark Lewis Taylor, eds. *Reconstructing Christian Theology* (Minneapolis, Minnesota: Fortress Press, 1994), 102.
10. Thich Nhat Hanh, *Living Buddah, Living Christ* (New York: Riverhead Books/ G. P. Putnam's Sons, 1995), 1769.
11. Macrina Wiederkehr, *A Tree Full of Angels* (San Fransisco: Harper Collins, 1988), 18.
12. From an old camp song.

13. John M. Krumm, *The Art of Being a Sinner* (New York: The Seabury Press, 1967), 71.

14. Alan Richardson, *The Bible in the Age of Science* (London: SCM Press, 1961), 156.

15. *The Art of Being a Sinner*, 72.

16. Jeffery Hopper in Donald W. Musser and Joseph L. Price, eds. *A New Handbook of Christian Theology* (Nashville, Tennessee: Abingdon Press, 1992), 454.

Chapter 4

 in Forgiveness

Too Good to Be True
By Geoff Spencer

> *If you forgive people enough you belong to them, and they to you,*
> *whether either person likes it or not—squatter's rights of the heart.*[1]

After languishing in obscurity, even disrepute, during the years when a facile optimism convinced human beings in the Western world that inevitable progress would lead to the kingdom of God, the notion of sin has returned with a vengeance. The appealing idea that tragedy, evil, and suffering would gradually be eliminated by education, goodwill, and intelligence now seems incredibly naïve.

Nevertheless, although the evidence of inhumanity, violence, hostility, and self-centeredness virtually overwhelms us, sin remains the one subject that people claim expert knowledge on the basis of other people's experience rather than their own. The widespread tendency may be to confess small faults, oversights, momentary lapses, but nothing that amounts to sin of major proportion. That is reserved for other people. At the worst, we might like to be considered "social" sinners, much as some people might admit to being "social drinkers," a small foible, but nothing to be upset about.

It would be very convenient to be able to allocate sin to the ill-mannered, the despicable, or the depraved, or to those who really offend us personally. This would then allow the rest of us to be known as very nice people—decent, honorable, and laden with virtue. We often unconsciously reveal our "innocence complex" in unintentional ways. I, like many others, have found myself exclaiming, "I just don't know what got into me; that's not like me at all," to dismiss a questionable or shameful act—but never to account for a piece of worthy or commendable behavior.

In the same fashion, if people acknowledge the need for forgiveness, it may well be for small offenses—lateness for an appointment, a momentary show of impatience, an unintended oversight. Beyond that, forgiveness has rarely enjoyed good press. It's bad enough to be preoccupied with sin, the argument runs, without claiming that any reform we might attempt depends on some outside act such as forgiveness. If we are to enjoy a relationship with God, why not let it be on the basis of our merits, strengths, and inherent goodness (see Luke 18:9–14), by which even God might be impressed? I suspect the traditional RLDS discomfort with the notion of justification by faith—even though the Inspired Version adds *"alone"* (Romans 8:31 IV)—stems not only from its Protestant overtones, but from our own preoccupation with good works as the ground for salvation.

For many Christians, what cannot be denied can be minimized—by a kind of justification by rationalization. The capacity to excuse ourselves is virtually inexhaustible, one of the most finely honed achievements known among human beings. It does not require too much of a stretch of the imagination—after all, we encounter self-justification on a daily basis. But consider how this might appear to someone with the capacity to see the sum total of such behavior, or to understand what this might look like extended into some form of afterlife:

> **It would be an appalling prospect: an eternity of millions of human creatures, all anxiously and nervously promoting themselves and insisting on their own importance. It would be difficult to imagine a situation more desperate than an endless lifetime of making excuses, trying to justify one's mistakes, bolstering one's reputation, proving over and over again one's superiority and virtue. Such an existence could only be described as hell—which is exactly what the classical theologies called it.[2]**

To be relieved of this burden of self-justification—this form of living hell, to use Krumm's painfully accurate metaphor—is the fruit of forgiveness, according to the Christian witness. But even if we can bring ourselves to the point of accepting this astonishing gift ourselves, the responsibility for forgiving others may then constitute an unwelcome and intolerable burden. Once again, at first glance, there would appear to be little prospect of joy. The notion of forgiving others, whatever we profess with our lips, may loom strange, even unacceptable. Once perhaps, twice under special circumstances; but seventy times seven, unthinkable (see Matthew 18:22).

In the first place, it may seem pointless, a futile expenditure of generosity and forbearance. A traditional Japanese proverb reflects this judgment: "Forgiving the unrepentant is like drawing pictures on water." That is to say, there's neither benefit nor future in it. Would it not make more sense, and be more productive (worthy of our forgiveness) if there were some signs of confession of indebtedness, sorrow, mended ways, restitution? However, it needs to be kept in mind that "while we were *yet* sinners, Christ died for us" (Romans 5:8). Repentance *follows* forgiveness and is a response to it, rather than a condition of it. One of the many "scandals" of Christianity is the assertion, plainly, that forgiveness, apart from the confession of faith, is unconditional.

On the other hand, many ever-sober, God-fearing Christians insist that forgiveness without some clear evidence of repentance is unethical, to say the least. Surely we should be required to give some evidence that we have *earned* our forgiveness, that God *owes* it to us. This is very close to the notion of forgiveness for merit: when one has measured up, then forgiveness may be extended. But this would confront us with Paul's dilemma: How was he, or any one of the rest of us, to be assured that our repentance had been sufficiently meritorious to merit forgiveness? (See Romans 7, the pivotal point in Paul's exposition of the gospel.) Any minister of long standing must be aware of the sense of guilt and unworthiness that hounds many people even in the midst of their best efforts, as if no amount of repentance could ever "win" the free gift of God's grace. Justification *by merit* has left a terrible legacy.

Another caution comes to mind. Jesus advised that we should "do good to those who despitefully use you (Luke 6:26–30/6:27–29 IV; see also Matthew 5:44/5:46 IV)." But does this not leave us open to continual abuse, being taken advantage of, at the mercy of everyone's shortcomings—in short, one of life's victims? What advantage, let alone joy, can surface under such conditions? Yet consider another possibility. Stephen Covey relates the story of a family torn apart by dissension and recrimination. One of the members confessed the pain and bitterness, the feeling of victimization at what had developed as a "family history." When this person took the initiative, at some risk, to restore a better relationship, the pain was replaced by the joy of forgiveness and peace."[3] Covey drew on this experience to conclude that "you will always be a victim until you forgive." So long as we carry grievances, harbor resentment, feel unjustly dealt with—our rights and privileges infringed upon—we shall suffer the role of the victim, of little value either to ourselves or to the "offender."

On one occasion Jesus specified that forgiveness should be "from the heart," indicating a feeling and inward attitude as well as an alteration of behavior toward the offender. Forgiveness that is reluctantly extended or given with a sense of virtue can hardly merit the name. With this understanding, let us consider the nature of forgiveness, and from this perspective discern how joy might ensue as a byproduct. Forgiveness has been described in the following way:

> **The active and intentional process by which an offended person (or community) takes the initiative to heal the breach, accept the offender, restore the relationship, and open the door to a renewed moral response.[4]**

Despite some discomfort with and even resistance to the principle embedded in Doctrine and Covenants 150:10–11, its demonstrated validity has enhanced our capacity to be a forgiving people. Individuals who may have been judged to be living in ignorance and below their potential will always need others prepared to "bear the burden of their sin," and this surely without any guarantee of a positive outcome. This is clearly the meaning of forgiveness—it is *fore-giveness*, extended in advance, because of the possibilities thereby opened up.

In this respect we will readily admit that we *all* stand, or have stood, in this position. Who among us has been so stalwart in virtue and complete in wisdom that at no time have we needed a sympathetic, forbearing presence to bear the burden of our sins, nurture us in the faith, and accept whatever degree of repentance was in us? I have long remembered a statement that appeared as part of the introduction to a movie I once saw: "If there is any similarity between the characters depicted in this film and any living characters, then those living characters ought to be ashamed of themselves." I have wondered many times whether any person, myself included, could have walked out of that movie without some very sobering thoughts. We truly would have been deceiving ourselves to claim there was no sin in us.

To be assured of forgiveness sets us free to deal with the past in a new way. This does not mean that the past can be changed, but we can change the way we deal with it. Donald Evans, in a masterly study titled *Struggle and Fulfillment,* describes the positive, even joyful response to the experience of being forgiven:

> **You don't have to impose suffering, or service, or scrupulosity on yourself in order to feel acceptable. Let the energies which are now trapped in conflict within you be released in you so that you may begin a new life.... The issue is whether an accusing, condemning voice of an alleged God pervades my life, crushing me or impelling me to futile and destructive attempts at atonement, or whether I hear and identify with the accepting voice of God so that I am continually liberated and converted and renewed.[5]**

That I can experience such freedom and acceptance is a source of joy. In such a relationship, free from self-righteousness on the one hand and unresolved guilt on the other, I am empowered to extend forgiveness to others in the hope that the relationship may open up ways for them to find the same joy and freedom. As the English novelist James Hilton has pointed out, forgiveness establishes a kind of "squatter's rights of the heart," by which forgiver and forgiven experience a new relationship, with no barriers to inhibit new possibilities.

Surely this is the whole purpose of a gift that seems too good to be true. Those who have experienced forgiveness become agents of the new reality that enters the world, as agents of reconciliation (see II Corinthians 5:17–21). Thus Krumm captures the vision of a forgiven and repentant community:

> **Being sorry opens up wells of concern and compassion and sympathy within the self and generates the grace and magnanimity which are so necessary in a society where men have sinned against each other for so long and can live together only on the basis of mutual forgiveness... .The Church represents that new depth in human community.[6]**

A community of disciples committed to peace, reconciliation, and healing of the spirit cannot do otherwise than affirm the promise of that calling, and sense the joy that comes from practicing the power of forgiveness. Such a community would indeed be "a great and marvelous work" (Doctrine and Covenants 6:1a). Both as individuals, and as part of the community, we may well rejoice in the gift that may appear to be too good to be true, but which nevertheless is fully true and trustworthy.

Joy and Forgiveness
By Crystal Crownover

My testimony is not the finding of joy in forgiveness, but rather finding forgiveness through joy. My life has been filled with joy from many sources. Music has played a major role. I loved to sing and direct the choir. I was blessed with opportunities for leadership in teaching, youth activities, and both local and regional retreats. My greatest joys, however, have come through people. I have been blessed with close and fulfilling relationships with siblings, children, grandchildren, and friends.

When one of the most significant relationships of my life was destroyed, I was overwhelmed with bitterness and pain. I chose to withdraw from all activities that were constant reminders of that pain.

For several years my only church fellowship was away from home. One beautiful autumn day, in the middle of the Missouri countryside, with the support of twenty caring women, I made a decision that I could no longer remain alienated. On my return home, I began a long, slow journey of return to the joy of fellowship and participation. Those who loved me stood by me and never gave up hope.

The more I became involved, the more my feelings of hurt and pain diminished. The first change I consciously noted I labeled "neutrality." I looked on my previous relationships without emotion—either positive or negative. As my participation moved toward the joys of accepting leadership, my feelings moved toward friendship and forgiveness. This has truly been a journey well-traveled.

The Only Way Home
By Frank Kelley

> *To be faithful means to be inwardly united with others in a relationship that puts us above all trivialities of daily life.*[7]

It had been a serious, loud, and vituperative time in the family kitchen. I stalked upstairs, resplendent in all the resentful indignation possible for a seven year old. A special, quiet time in the bathroom, glaring at the angry mirror and dreaming of final victory and revenge, firmed the conviction that the time had come to leave, escape, just go away, leaving all this oppression and tribulation behind. Forever! Stealing into my parent's bedroom, I took a dollar bill from mother's purse and slipped out of the house. I knew where to go to have the best, unfettered time of all.

West on Huntoon Street, about two blocks, was a small one-room restaurant. Great, celestial-level hamburgers were produced in greasy glory. Adding to the delights, the place was furnished with a pinball machine. Wolfing down a burger with everything, swilling a Royal Crown Cola, and slamming the shiny steel balls around the glittering board, I knew I had escaped into a far country, was squandering my inheritance, and loved it. Neither the cook with the filthy apron, nor the shoe repairman from next door, sipping a root beer in the corner of the place, dared inquire as to my newfound wealth and bold enjoyment. They recognized true freedom when they saw it.

Sated, I left the place and stepped into the cool, Kansas evening.

I heard the cicadas singing in the elms. I also heard my mother's voice as she strode up the street. Following a portentous walk home, I got to cut a switch from our mulberry tree, and we entered the house. The party was over. The mulberry switch was utilized with more than enough enthusiasm, I thought. And then my mother laid face down on the bed and wept.

If it had been my father acting as witness, judge, jury, and executioner in all this, I would have suffered several dozen differing accounts of the episode—shared with selected others—well into at least my fourth decade. Forgetting was not a skill he ever mastered. Mother, however, embodied a special blend of justice and mercy. Justice was swift and sure. Mercy was extended in the fact that no further mention of any of this trouble was ever made. She loved her children, brooked no nonsense, and carried no baggage. Forgiveness was a given.

That terrible afternoon inspired a lesson I have carried for more than fifty years: the events were the guarantor of her love, the warranty of her forgiveness. The joy and impress of that experience have never completely left me. I realized love and experienced forgiveness in such power that I determined never again to do anything that would precipitate that hurt, that weeping. Of course, I am sure I did; but not, I hope, in any premeditated manner.

In like fashion, down the corridor of the years, I have experienced the presence of our heavenly Parent—the touch of the transcendent—in such a sweet embrace of loving forgiveness that in my best moments I desire nothing more than to never cause sorrow to such a One. And I know that the most genuine of all my relationships with the rest of God's family rest on such a mutual extension of care and grace. This mutuality and independence is at the heart of our Lord's instruction to the disciples that one seeks to be forgiven in the same manner in which one forgives. Thich Nhat Hanh writes: "We always postpone being alive to the future."[8] Forgiveness given and received is a source of joy—both today and through many tomorrows.

Notes

1.   James Hilton, *Time and Time Again*.

45

2. John M. Krumm, *The Art of Being a Sinner* (New York: The Seabury Press, 1967), 112.
3. Stephen R. Covey, *The 7 Habits of Highly Effective Families* (New York: Golden Books, 1997), 58–59.
4. Geoffrey Spencer, *Strangers and Pilgrims* (Independence, Missouri: Herald House, 1984), 90.
5. Donald Evans, *Struggle and Fulfillment* (Cleveland, Ohio: Collins, 1979), 118.
6. *The Art of Being a Sinner*, 74, 78.
7. Albert Schweitzer, *Reverance for Life* (New York: Harper and Row, 1969), 84.
8. Thich Nhat Hanh, *Living Buddah, Living Christ* (New York: Riverhead Books, 1995), 17.

Chapter 5

The  of Community

Where Two or Three Are Gathered
By Barbara Howard

The potbellied stove of the small, white church building ("Little Church," we called it) glowed with welcoming heat. Winters in Mobile, Alabama, could be bitterly cold. I was dressed in my Sunday finery, with the final touch—a white rabbit fur coat, hat, and muff. Shirley Temple wore one in a movie and lots of six- to eight-year- old girls had them. But despite the fur coat I was cold and stood with my back to the stove, visiting my friends and letting the heat warm me through and through.

I thought my parents would be furious, that the kids would make fun of me, that I'd be humiliated and disgraced, but instead, all was well. The next week, there was a protective screen around the stove. If a coat could burn from the heat's intensity, so could a child who might stumble or just get too close.

This may be my first conscious awareness of something that many years later would be named "grace." I knew unconditional, accepting love. That congregation, diverse in age, filled with loving Southern folk who also carried all the baggage of years of prejudice and fear, loved me and called out my gifts. Children were valued, given opportunity to serve, to discover talents, to make mistakes. It was my larger family: inclusive in ages, economics, and to some extent theologically, but certainly not racially.

In the ensuing years, with the advent of World War II and other family concerns, our family became inactive until the spring of 1944, my fourteenth year. Returning to church after inactivity, even if the memories were wonderful, was difficult. The young people had their own inner circle and I felt left out. For several Sundays I would leave church after the closing hymn and sit in the car until my folks finished their after-church visiting and decided to leave.

One Sunday, just as we were leaving, Henry Porter, the youth leader, came over to the car. "We're going on a youth retreat in Pensacola on Friday. Have Barbara at the bus station at five o'clock. Without asking me anything, Mother replied, "She'll be there."

The retreat, with guest ministers Maurice and Ruth Draper, was life-changing for me. I found my community drawing me in again, loving me into being, offering opportunities for growth. Consequently, attending Graceland College flowed naturally from the understanding that the church called me to develop skills, to learn, to mature.

Community is inclusive

Although I was bright enough to avoid standing by a hot stove in a fur coat, I had much to learn. At a meal in the basement of Walker Hall, I shared genuine communion with Mattie Willis, a black Saint from Michigan. I can still remember seeing her black hand and my white hand reach for the salt shaker at the same time. At that time in parts of the United States black and white people did not break bread together. In that moment my mind and heart expanded. And so did my concept of God.

My childish understandings of a white, RLDS, male (and yes, Southern) English-speaking God, showed me that we sometimes "create God in our own image," and God, who loves us so much, shatters those images so that we are free. My limited views of God continue to be shattered and I pray this may always be so. How can I participate in a worldwide, multiracial, multicultural community without changing my narrow views? There are dangers in exclusive communities. It is easy to feel certain that the way the community views the world is the "only" and "right" way. When this attitude persists the group develops a feeling of superiority. Sharon Welch in her recent book, *Sweet Dreams in America,* writes: "What maintains delusions of certainty and group superiority? Insularity. What enables foundational critiques of one's own society? Difference."[1]

Certainly those different from me have opened my heart and mind in ways for which I shall be forever grateful. A healthy church community reflects a population of all races, economic levels, educational levels, sexual preferences, ages, skills, interests, and abilities. Our church community is only as strong and healthy as its differences.

Adults who serve on the staff of camps designed for special needs children such as cancer patients or cystic fibrosis patients are nearly always changed by their contact with children they thought might be weak and needy, only to discover strength and faith that challenged their own.

Building community is the most creative and difficult work to which any of us will ever be called. There is no higher achievement in all the world than to be a person in community, and this is the call of every Christian. We are to be builders of liberating communities that free love in us and free love in others.

In the sixties and seventies the church suffered from a desire on the part of various interest groups to have the community be a monolithic body. Differing points of view were unacceptable. What a joy the 1994 World Conference was as the delegates struggled with the issue of open Communion, and expressed widely divergent views. Today, as we struggle with difficult issues such as rebaptism and homosexuality, we are encouraged to dialogue rather than debate. Changing our own viewpoints, avoiding judgment of those who disagree, and listening to one another can create a wonderfully safe environment for the gospel to be lived out as we struggle with issues together. M. Scott Peck writes in *The Different Drum:*

> **Community is and must be inclusive. The great enemy of community is exclusivity. Groups that exclude others because they are poor or doubters or divorced or sinners or of some different race or nationality are not communities; they are cliques— actually defensive bastions against community.**[2]

Community offers safety

I have experienced liberating community in many settings throughout the church, but particularly at women's retreats, which are often exclusively for women and reflect a wide range of population, interests, and ages. One retreat that stands out was one in which two young mothers who were nursing their babies brought the infants to retreat. The dynamics changed with the presence of the children. Women responded immediately to the needs of the mothers and of the infants. In one of the worship services during a time of silence one of the babies began to cry. As that cry pierced the silence, I noticed tears in the eyes of many women. Later, during a time of sharing, one of the women said, "When Allison began to cry, I thought of the hungry children of the world and vowed to be more proactive in the fight against world hunger." There was no criticism of the child or her mother. In this safe environment the infant was a gift liberating the group from a narrow focus to a broader view of God's needy world.

Women's groups have often been the one safe place for women who have been violated. At every retreat I have ever attended, at least one woman has told her story of abuse. Sometimes the stories have been so harrowing that the only adequate response is silence, but always these women know they are safe and embraced.

Prayer services in my present congregation provide such a safe community. People can bring their heartaches, the deepest needs of their lives, and sometimes intimate concerns, and the community holds their confidence, embraces the pain, and supports them with prayers and outreach ministries. While the community at prayer service is not the entire congregation, I believe the entire body is enriched by the level of compassion and trust expressed on those Wednesday nights.

I have felt loved and cherished in our community here in Florida even though I know that many of my views are different from those of some of my closest friends. Being with people who think differently has taught me to listen, but I have not felt anyone trying to change me. This is a priceless gift—one I wished I had practiced earlier in my life.

Community calls forth gifts

In the book *The Man Who Mistook His Wife for a Hat,* the neurologist and neurosurgeon Oliver Sachs describes a woman who came to the hospital where he works.

She had severe cerebral palsy. Because she was blind and came from a family of unlimited wealth, she had always been waited on and had never known deprivation because of the disease. She came to the hospital because she had no feeling in her hands. After countless tests and examinations, Sachs determined that there was nothing neurologically wrong with her. She had just never used her hands. He persuaded the nurses and her attendants to set her food just a bit out of reach so that she might try to grasp with her hands, but they were never to let her go hungry. One day, extremely busy, the staff forgot to check on her. She became hungry enough to lunge out at her tray and grasp a bagel. That bagel became to her what water was to Helen Keller. It was the first thing she had ever truly felt. From that moment on she wanted to touch everything. In six month's time she asked for clay and began to sculpt the things she felt. She became known as the "Blind Sculptress of St. Benedict's." Sachs asks:

Who could have dreamed that in this blind, palsied woman, hidden away, inactivated, over-protected all her life, there lay the gem of an astonishing artistic sensibility . . that would germinate and blossom into a rare and beautiful reality, after remaining dormant, blighted, for sixty years?[3]

This story calls to mind my experience in the church community. There have always been challenges put out just a little beyond my reach, and I have been able to discover gifts I never realized were mine until placed in the environment of challenge.

I was privileged to serve on the committee that developed the hymnal published in 1981, *Hymns of the Saints*. It was a model for the ideal committee as well as a paradigm for community. Harold Neal, with the assistance of some others, selected a group of people with a wide range of musical abilities and theological backgrounds. I was the only member of the committee who could not read music, but I was a full participant. I brought a writing background and a deep appreciation for poetry and language. I would sometimes sit in awe as members of the committee discussed concerns about music. I would often not be certain what they were saying, but I knew when we sang if a tune was very difficult, or if the words didn't fit the melody, or if the melody didn't match the tone of the hymn.

Everyone on the committee was a leader. Every person's opinion mattered. Discussions were lively and sometimes heated. Out of that seven-year experience I discovered a deep interest in hymnody and wrote several texts. So did Barbara Higdon, Geoffrey Spencer, Alan Tyree, and Peter Judd. Rosalee Elser used her extensive skills in music to do some magnificent harmonizations. Each meeting brought fruitful results from members of the committee, and we had so much fun. I've often thought about the Saturday and Sunday meetings and how energized I felt after the long hours we spent together. I would like to believe that what happened in our committee is a microcosm of the church at its finest—each member is valued and encouraged to develop unique skills. The entire body benefits when this happens.

Community requires vulnerability

We sat facing each other in an exercise at a congregational retreat. Our assignment: share a fear you keep from others. This was difficult and required some soul-searching. As I struggled to reveal one of my secret fears I looked into my partner's eyes and realized that he was resisting the exercise. "You're not comfortable, are you?" I asked. "No," he said. "And I'm not going to tell you anything about me."

We were not partners during the class session. He lived in his world, and although I had shared myself, I didn't feel comfortable because he was neither interested in my fears nor did he want to hear about them.

We did not experience community that day. The love and freedom that reside at the heart of genuine community could not be expressed: "for in love two unique beings undergo a transformation through what each gives and receives, and this always involves a threat to the self as it is."[4] To overcome this threat a person must be willing to be vulnerable to another. Such trust is foundational to community.

I experienced a completely different environment in 1993 at the International Women's Conference held in Independence, Missouri, as a Temple dedicatory event. I worked at Herald House that week and attended the conference as a reporter as well as a participant. Between sessions it was not uncommon to see a small group of women sitting together sharing intimately. Sometimes one of the women would be weeping and the others would be holding her hand. I heard countless stories of shared grief, of healing support, of shared joy, and healing laughter. On the Saturday night as the women encircled the Temple with lighted candles, there was an incredible power of community expressed in the sharing of banners, in the sharing of lives:

> **Vulnerability is a two-way street. Community requires the ability to expose our wounds and weaknesses to our fellow creatures. It also requires the capacity to be affected by the wounds of others, to be wounded by their wounds.[5]**

Years ago I heard someone speak about the word "bioluminescence," a phenomenon off the south shore of Puerto Rico. The surf carries an incredible light that comes from thousands of protozoa. When one tiny protozoa comes in contact with another, the nerves of one trigger the light of the other. They must touch each other in order for the light to shine.

We need each other. Remembering the protozoa, let the prophet Isaiah encourage us to be vulnerable to one another and create a community of joy, hope, love, and peace: "Arise, shine; for your light has come, and the glory of the Lord has risen upon you" (Isaiah 60:1 RSV).

Beloved Community of God
By Geoff Spencer

In some sense... freedom to be left alone is a freedom that implies being alone.[6]

Perhaps freedom is the most resonant, deeply held value by Americans, states Robert Bellah and his associates in their extensive study of contemporary culture and character in the United States of America. It is very likely a similar value would be accorded primacy in a number of other democratically governed nations. However, they point out, it is not a value without its perplexities:

> **What it is that one might do with that freedom is much more**

difficult for Americans to define. And if the entire social world is made up of individuals, each endowed with the right to be free of other's demands, it becomes hard to forge bonds of attachment to, or cooperation with, other people, since such bonds would imply obligations that necessarily impinge on one's freedom.[7]

There is, at the same time, an abundance of evidence to show that Americans have also benefited from the influence of collective traditions, that still exert a powerful drawing power. Such traditions were expressed among many of the early immigrants to the new land, infusing religious, social, and political life in the new colonies. Even now, I am astonished at the seemingly endless variety of special interest groups, clubs, and organizations through which Americans seek the experience of intimacy and attempt to compensate for the compartmentalization that our highly efficient societal system appears to require.

Although the term "community" is a relatively recent addition to our vocabulary, the roots of the image go deep in our RLDS tradition. It explains, in part, why the concept of Zion simply refuses to go away, evoking as it does the hope of a blessed community under God. Although the index of topics in *The Hymnal* (1956) included no reference to "community," as compared to twenty in *Hymns of the Saints* (1981), this arises from a development in our language rather than any change in our sentiments and deeply held commitments. The faith by which I endeavor to live my life is not a privately held, privately cultivated, and privately enjoyed possession. I am inescapably part of a community.

Early in my life, before I had the language to describe it, I was the beneficiary of such community. This was partly due to the circumstances of the times, but more so because of the expressed power of community in the small congregation in which I grew up. During the war years, gasoline restrictions meant that virtually no family in the congregation owned a motor vehicle. Our first service began at mid-afternoon every Sunday, followed by an evening service at 7:00 p.m. My family, like most of the others, lived too far from the premises we rented for church to travel home, eat, and return for this evening service. Even had time permitted, the cost of public transportation home and back again for a family of five would have strained our meager financial resources. And so we ate the evening meal at the "church," along with most of the other families. We spent as many as six hours together every Sunday. As I have indicated elsewhere, for much of the time I was growing up there were no others my own age. The members of the congregation became my extended family, friends, and mentors. They created opportunities for me to gain experience and encouraged me in my efforts without judgment. I recall that as an eighteen year old and serving as music director, I was "allowed" by them to write some words and music for choir items that we incorporated into the congregation's worship. I know those efforts would not stand up to any discerning music critic today, but the congregation made no effort to belittle my venture—and, blessedly, it (the music, not the congregation) has been consigned to oblivion.

In that "beloved community" I was given every opportunity to learn, make mistakes, grow, and have experiences that would have been virtually impossible in a larger congregation. Looking back over the years, I can only assume that I took for granted what surely must be one of the most precious gifts people can bestow on each other—the gift of unconditional acceptance and trust. My initial call to ordination occurred in my thirteenth year. Unknown to me, it had been the intention of the pastor to initiate the call a year earlier, but my parents, when consulted, expressed the wish for me to be granted another year of childhood freedom. I needed the time, though the "freedom" might not have always been expressed judiciously. Just one week before the call was eventually considered in the branch I had indulged in a childish "prank" (even the memory of it embarrasses me) that might well have disposed the Saints to conclude some further time for maturing would not go astray. Nevertheless, the members of the congregation placed their faith in me both in their vote of approval and their subsequent mentoring of me and the other young person called and ordained at the same time. From that initial ordination to ministry until I was ordained an elder eight years later, very shortly before leaving to teach in rural high schools, this was my primary community. In a very real sense I was a living embodiment of the wisdom that "it takes a whole village to raise a child."

From the advantage of hindsight, and in view of our current emphasis on the Saints moving out into the broader community, it could be said that my world was too small, too restricted, too ingrown, and sheltered. And yet, I believe it was this community, and its closeness, that gave me the sense of confidence and self-worth so important for my future life.

Yet another dimension of community nurturing was a sense of responsibility against which I sometimes rebelled. One of my mother's favorite sayings, repeated, I thought, at the most discomforting times, was, "There are no menial tasks in the service of the Lord." I could agree with this in principle, but when it came to specific tasks to be performed, I often had the feeling that I was, so to speak, cursed with a sense of obligation. There were occasions when I was moved to respond on no more praiseworthy ground than that I owed it to the community that had invested so much in me.

This sense of community broadened as I served in three assignments under World Church appointment in Australia, and it has continued ever since. In some ways it faced its first real test during my initial assignment in the United States, when it became evident that some folk held and expressed widely differing views about the "new curriculum," even questioning my worthiness to be a part of the community. Nevertheless, the power of that community, even when all were not necessarily of the same mind, was strong enough, at least for me, to transcend any possible adverse impact. In the ensuing years the abiding power of the community has been confirmed and reinforced for me in virtually every part of the United States and among the Saints wherever I have traveled throughout the missions of the church.

I am in no position to judge how others experience their lives without some sense of community and commitment through which to share their patterns of involvement and relationships with others. If, as suggested by Robert Bellah and his associates, freedom may well imply freedom to be lonely, without limiting ties or obligations, then I consider it a blessing to be tied and obligated. I am intrigued, even disbelieving, when I read of Henry David Thoreau's preference:

I never found the companion that was so companionable as solitude. We are for the most part more lonely when we go abroad among men than when we stay in our chambers. A man thinking or working is always alone, let him be where he will.[8]

I value opportunities for solitude and retreat, and there are times and situations when I think more easily, though not necessarily more fruitfully, alone. Yet virtually all of the activities that make up my life are enhanced, balanced, and given their richness and texture in the company of others who share my values, commitments, and dreams.

Notes

1. Sharon Welch, *Sweet Dreams in America: Making Ethics and Spirituality Work* (New York: Routledge, 1998), 67.
2. M. Scott Peck, *The Different Drum: Community-Making and Peace* (New York: Simon and Schuster, 1987), 61.
3. Oliver Sachs, *The Man Who Mistook His Wife for a Hat* (New York: Harper and Row, 1985), 59–65.
4. Daniel Day Williams, *The Spirit and the Forms of Love* (New York: Harper and Row, 1968), 115.
5. Peck, 70.
6. Robert N. Bellah, et. al., *Habits of the Heart: Individualism and Commitment in American Life* (Berkeley, California: University of California, 1985), 23.
7. Ibid.
8. Henry David Thoreau (1817–1862), "Solitude."

Chapter 6

 in Times of Transition

First the Trial, Then the Blessing
By Frank Kelley

All change in habits of life and of thought is irksome.[1]

It was a Wednesday evening, about half past seven. We had gathered in the little house that we called our church home for prayer meeting. The minister, an elder new to our group, announced the hymn ("Let us Pray for One Another"). He then loosed the furies. Announcing that we would *individually stand* in our places to pray, rather than kneel together as was our custom, the house of the Lord was transformed instantly into a center of confusion and resentment.

Although this historic event took place in the mid-1940s, it has been replicated countless times to the present. One has only to substitute a particular form or practice with a different one for some degree of social pyrotechnics to be almost guaranteed. Such reaction is not limited to church traditions. Indeed, it appears that resistance to change is found somewhere buried in the human genes. Discomfort with change can be traced at least as far back as Heracletus,[2] who declared with great finality, "There is nothing permanent except change." This, however, was a position destined for rejection for centuries—indeed, almost to the present day.

Only in recent years have I come to terms with the understanding that change—transition, if you will—is our fixed course. Nurtured since conception by Restoration word and expectation, I successfully ignored the repeated proclamation that "a marvelous work is about to come forth," a promise of things new and different if ever there was one.

Oft-quoted popular sources and thinkers have trumpeted change as the hallmark of our age. Jawaharlal Nehru in 1958 wrote: "The basic fact of today is the tremendous pace of change in human life."[3] The concept of paradigm shifts is now practically a cliché, but in the early 1990s it was seen as an important and insightful tool, helpful in understanding the process and effect of transitions. Paul Kennedy, in a best-selling analysis of these times, concluded, "The pace and complexity of the forces for change are enormous and daunting."[4]

Peace with the present, and a particular aspect of joy, have been my companions since accepting the constancy of change—the realization that transition is our blessing, not our bane. A friend sent me a quotation (source unknown) from J. Robert Oppenheimer:

To assail the changes that have unmoored us from the past is futile, and in a deep sense, I think it is wicked.... This cannot be an easy life. We shall have a rough time of it to keep our minds open, and to keep them deep... in a great, open, windy world; but this is, as I see it, the condition of man; and in this condition we can help, because we can love one another.

I shudder to think what might have been had we never stood to pray, had we never produced another hymnal, had we not printed a "new" curriculum, had our sisters never been allowed to don the mantle of ministry. Robert Grudin tells us: "All important actions are open-ended to the future."[5] Who is to say, in the complexity of a given moment, what actions are important? Who can guess what amazing and interesting future awaits us?

Praise God, who told us he was going to do a new thing, whose Son blessed us by making all things new, and whose constantly present Spirit always leads us toward the next marvelous thing about to come forth. There is great, transcendent joy in becoming. Robert Louis Stevenson was dead right when he told us that "To travel hopefully is a better thing than to arrive."[6] And Mary Oliver, poet and artist with words, said it well: "I don't want to end up simply having visited this world."[7]

Always Another Adventure
By Donna Sperry

It is not always with joy that I have experienced the transitions of my life. Having been born in the age of the "baby boomers," I have been part of a generation that has experienced a great deal of transition. I used to struggle against each one, wondering why I always had to break new ground in the movements of my life. As I moved into adulthood in the late sixties and early seventies I entered a culture in chaos. Fundamental questions were being asked about who we were to be in the world. At the same time I was entering the world of medicine as a nurse and as a woman. Feminism caused me to explore deeper issues of what my role was to be in life as a woman and a nurse. Both roles were to undergo complete structural changes in the years to come.

Life in the church has been equally fraught with change and uncertainty. I have gone from being told at sixteen that women were not even to read scriptures in a pre-worship service to now holding a full-time position as a Transformation 2000 minister. And what a journey that has been! Other transitions in the church have demanded that I explore my own beliefs more fully and take responsibility for increasing my knowledge in the Christian life.

As I occasionally allowed myself some frustration over these myriad changes, I was impressed by my mother-in-law's response to multiple, and often difficult, transitions in her own life. Her standard response was, "Well, I guess I am in for another adventure!" Hearing her make that statement over an ever-increasing array of circumstances changed my own attitude. I began to see with new eyes the gift that the transitions of my life had offered me.

Life as an adventure carries with it the most wonderful possibilities. There is certainly loss as well. Some of those losses are to be mourned, some are to be celebrated. But transitions give us an opportunity for new beginnings. We can have a part in creating what will evolve from those beginnings and experience the joy of being engaged in a brand-new process.

My most recent transition, that of leaving a career in nursing to one in full-time ministry, looms as large as my original coming of age in the late sixties. This transition has brought with it all the same fears and uncertainties, questions and speculations, hopes and joys I felt as a young woman trying to make my way in the world of adulthood and medicine. But a full life of transitions has helped me to gain a new perspective on the experience. There is a deep, abiding joy that comes in the midst of creating something new. There is an underlying confidence that comes from knowing that a life in the midst of change is supported and upheld by the presence of the Divine. There is promise in the awareness that as we move in response to a sense of call, God will go before us and will be with us in our moving.

It is with great joy that I now embrace the transitions of my life. They still carry with them a degree of uncertainty and disorientation, but I believe Christ calls us to walk through that uncertainty toward a new tomorrow. I can now joyfully proclaim for myself, "I guess I am in for another adventure!"

How Did I Get Here from There?
By Geoff Spencer

Since joining the staff of a large East Coast newspaper some years ago, our older son, Paul, has received several promotions, and is presently one of the two managing editors and part of the supervising team. Recently he said to me, "Dad, the longer I stay with this paper the further away I get from what I was trained to do." He went on to say that having prepared to report news, he now supervised production, personnel, budgets, and other matters related to the general success of the paper.

It required no manipulation of the facts to say I knew exactly what he was talking about. I had begun as a teacher, functioned briefly as a school counselor, then as a missionary elder under World Church appointment telling, like my son, the good news, even on occasion knocking on doors to tell it. At the time of retirement I spent a considerable proportion of my time and energy supervising a staff, considering the allocation of personnel, working with budgets, and discussing with other general officers of the church matters of general policy and procedure. The cynic might say I was a living example of the rule known as the "Peter Principle": one is "promoted" until one reaches one's level of incompetence!

And yet my story is similar to a large proportion of people in our contemporary society, differing only in the details. We are a very "moving" people, not only in terms of where we live but in terms of what we "do." We are not so far from the time when many people would live and work where their fathers had lived and worked, and where they expected their sons to live and work. That situation seems to belong to a bygone age, not so remote in time as in our ability to conceive of that life style. Most of us will go through several transitions—some planned and anticipated, others without warning and perhaps unwelcomed. It is to be hoped most of those transitions will be acceptable and satisfying, but not necessarily so. And so most of us may well ask, "How did I get here from there?"

Such a question might have occurred to the Israelites on the banks of the Red Sea as they saw the Egyptian army bearing down on them (see Exodus 14:10–12). At that moment slavery in Egypt, offering a stable and familiar existence, must have loomed as an attractive alternative to the future promised by Moses. The work might have been burdensome—and the future without promise—but at least meals and accommodation were provided.

Not all of the transitions we might experience in the course of a lifetime will confront us with such drastic alternatives. Nevertheless, there will be elements of uncertainty about them. Even as a teacher, moving from a rural high school environment, with its close associations with other teachers, students, and parents, to the relatively impersonal world of a city high school, was a transition I did not adjust to easily. In the new environment the hours at school were completely separated from the rest of my life, with no connecting points of any kind. At the same time, I had married, so when Jill and I accepted World Church appointment, we found ourselves making the adjustment not only to this relationship but to the fact we were both leaving professions for which we had been trained, for the relatively unknown world of full-time church service in a strange city.

There were always elements of uncertainty in adjusting to the eight different assignments or roles that I experienced for the remainder of my life under appointment, including the transition to a culture that was considerably more different than may have appeared on the surface. It was not always in a humorous context that we referred to our initial assignment away from Australia as our first" foreign" assignment. But in each case there were serious questions. What if the new role didn't meet my preconceived expectations, or I didn't measure up? What if it called for skills that had not been tested? Given my inadequate theological education, would I find myself not competent for the task? It was this sense of inadequacy that pressed me once again back into the world of serious academic study and required the "resurrection" of skills that had essentially lain dormant for almost two decades. In later years, as the workplace became computerized, I faced with some difficulty a technological transition that some of my contemporaries found extremely daunting and to some degree, declined to make.

Each transition brought with it a change in the nature of the relationships I experienced "on the job." Invariably I had developed special feelings for those with whom I had been associated, and as much as I might have wished otherwise, the circumstances changed. In this sense I found that you can't go "home" again but must learn to inhabit a new dwelling place.

Perhaps for me the most demanding transition entailed my change from field apostle to president of the Council of Twelve. Although this may seem difficult to understand, there was a kind of loneliness about a role that could take me everywhere, without belonging anywhere. I came to understand that when members of the Council of Twelve referred to the members in their field as "my people" it was neither possessiveness nor paternalism, but rather an expression of the desire (need?) to experience the intimate relationship of the Saints—to belong.

On the day my release from appointment was announced, I discovered that I was to become a grandparent—and so the transitions continued. Over the next five years I undertook new family relationships, became a congregational presiding elder again for the first time in forty years, inhabited (too frequently for my preference) the world of hospitals and surgeries, and then returned again to the field of Christian education as a member of the Tri-Stake Mission Center staff. Each of these new circumstances has brought new dimensions to my life—some altogether fresh and unexplored, not all welcomed, and some beyond my control though necessary. And so it seems that it would be daring, even foolhardy, to believe I have come to the end of transitions, especially in light of the ultimate transition that awaits us all.

What this means for me is that there is an element of uncertainty, risk, hesitation, tentativeness in even the most eagerly anticipated and welcome of transitions. Yet to be quite truthful, I need to confess that every transition has brought with it a dimension of joy—for new opportunities, new associations, new challenges, a new place in the community committed to the mission of Christ in the world.

I might not always understand how I got here from there, but the journey—past, present, and to come—is a joyful venture.

Notes

1. Thorstein Veblin, *The Theory of the Leisure Class* (New York: MacMillan, Mentor), 136.
2. Heracletus: Fragment.
3. Jawaharlal Nehru, "Credo," *New York Times Magazine* (September 7, 1958).
4. Paul Kennedy, *Preparing for the Twenty-First Century* (New York: Random House, 1993), 349.
5. Robert Grudin, *Time and the Art of Living* (New York: Tichnor & Fields, 1982), 130.
6. Robert Louis Stevenson, *Bartlett's Familiar Quotations* (Boston: Little, Brown and Co., 1968), 822.
7. Mary Oliver, "When Death Comes."

Chapter 7

The  of Friendship

The Better Part of Ourselves
By Geoff Spencer

How often are we to die before we go quite off this stage? In every friend we lose part of ourselves, and the best part.[1]

As a young person growing up, I had very few close friends, if any. Whether this was influenced by genetic elements or by particular factors in my early life, I do not know. Due to circumstances that I would not recommend to anybody, I spent the greater part of my senior year in high school as a fifteen year old. Most of my classmates were one or two years older than me, and some even more than that. Even when I repeated that final year because I was not old enough to be admitted to the Faculty of Law at Sydney University, I still felt, in many respects, on my own, because I did know many of the incoming students. The fact that I was the only RLDS youth at a Methodist high school did nothing to relieve this feeling of isolation. I had many acquaintances, but no friends—a very private person.

I was ordained to the office of deacon at the age of thirteen, at the same time another young man in the congregation, somewhat older, was ordained. However, the time came when he was called into the military, and I was again in many ways alone. I appreciated those who served as mentors for me in the congregation but had, or took, very few steps to cultivate peer relationships at deeper levels.

To this day I can recall how easily my father appeared to make new friendships. Quite often traveling on the public transport to or from the congregations we attended he would engage people—

male or female, young or old—in conversation, very often listening to their problems, taking a note of their phone numbers, sharing encouragement. I envied his gift and yet was overcome with embarrassment at his apparent presumption in being so "forward."

This sense of apartness, of isolation, was essentially unchanged in my years at the university—again the only RLDS member among the entire student body, as far as I knew. As a teacher, essentially isolated from the church while teaching at rural high schools in New South Wales, I began to venture into some closer relationships. But in many cases differences in lifestyle and commitments erected barriers, and my involvement in the various denominations tended to accentuate the differences. Here, as hitherto, I might have cultivated significant relationships but had little experience or foundation on which to take the initiative.

When I did find myself experiencing the joy of a closer relationship, it was with a church member ten years my senior. My friendship with Paul continued and grew over the next fifty years, despite the fact that for the greater part of that time we were separated by almost 10,000 miles. Distance and the passage of time deepened the friendship. In some way that I do not understand, the relationship and sense of closeness continue after his death.

Neither Alexander Pope (1688–1744) nor Jonathan Swift (1667–1745) were the kind of men who appeared to seek or inspire friendship and were more likely to have repelled it. Pope has been accused of displaying a "detestable pettiness" and Swift was described by one associate as, at worst, a "brutal bully." Nevertheless Pope could confess, in a letter to Swift, that every loss of a friend was like a little death, and perhaps Swift, as biting, dominating, and intimidating as he could be, understood.

I believe I understand what Pope was trying to say. To lose a friend is to die a little, in some sense, within ourselves. I believe this to be more profound because it is also true that in our friends we perceive what we at our best would like to be. Perhaps that is why we are drawn to certain people in the first place, because we see or sense in them the embodiment of characteristics that seem so desirable and worthy of emulation. This I sense in my awareness of loss with Paul's death—and indeed in some respects the loss of my better self. This is true also as the passing years and advancing age remove from the scene others with whom I have come to feel a close affinity.

As I returned to closer geographic location with the church, and then accepted World Church appointment, I have learned to find joy in cultivating friendships, and have and do now enjoy many such relationships. I do not understand how Henry Brooks Adams could claim that "One friend in a lifetime is much; two are many; three are hardly possible."[2] Perhaps it is the close community of the church, where people share convictions, commitments, hopes, and dreams, that creates the environment in which the mutual trust and empathy so necessary to friendship are almost taken for granted.

Nor are all these friendships necessarily of long standing. One of the exciting elements I experience in visiting new jurisdictions is the possibility that a new friendship may be in the birthing. Perhaps as we become more aware of the promise of new friendships, we are more ready to make ourselves vulnerable to the risk of meeting another in a depth relationship. I can well remember that there was a time when only with the greatest safeguards would I venture to share even a little of myself.

At the time I was attending Sydney Teachers' College there was a story circulating, probably apocryphal, about a member of the faculty, a professor renowned for his interest in and concern for children. According to the story, the professor had just completed the laying of new concrete on his driveway when one of the small neighborhood children ran across the concrete, leaving footprints deeply embedded in the drying surface. The professor began to berate the child soundly, whereupon a next-door neighbor protested, saying: "But professor, how can you be so harsh? Everybody knows you love children." "Indeed I do," replied the professor, "but in the abstract, not on the concrete!"

As I reflect on those relationships that have ripened into friendship, I perceive that I was accepted "in the concrete," so to speak. If my experience is like that of others, then in the haste and complexity of our lives, many if not most of our associations, even those within the community of the church, result in me being experienced "in the abstract," as the administrator, staff person, instructor, or quorum member. This is not to disparage those relationships, only to acknowledge that given the lack of time or the absence of the right circumstances, such is the reality. It is when I am fortunate to be able to perceive another as he or she is, as a unique entity, and am seen in the same way, that the relationship can reach below the surface to its deeper dimensions.

Although the primary focus in Carl Rogers' book *On Becoming a Person* was not on friendship, I have long felt that several of the characteristics he examined have borne directly on the way such friendships are nurtured and sustained. Individuals may differ widely in background, education, interests, skills, even temperament, yet the closeness of a genuine friendship will transcend such differences, or any others that we might identify. The heart and sustainer of the friendship lies elsewhere.

In the first place, each person must be seen as **trustworthy**, not so much in terms of being rigidly consistent as in being dependably real. If I am to be a friend, do I understand my own feelings, attitudes, and motivations clearly enough so that, as far as possible, it is the genuine "I" who is available to another person and not some inconsistent representation of myself? This is a gift I have come to appreciate in my friends, so that I am encouraged and freed to offer the same gift in return. I do not need to be somebody other than who or what I am.

Second, and this has not always been easy for me, I believe it is important to have a sufficiently strong **sense of respect** in my own attitudes, convictions, and feelings that I can be healthily "separate" from the other person. The deepening of the friendship rests not only in my respect and consideration for the feelings and opinions of my friend, but also in my security to express my own self honestly. Unless it is my genuine self that is respectfully maintained, then it is a false closeness or unity that ensues.

Perhaps most important of all, I believe I need to meet another person as one in the process of **becoming**. My tendency, for obvious reasons, is to relate to others as they have been, on the basis of their past and my past. This may be no longer who they are, nor who I am, so that the relationship is founded on a reality that no longer exists. This has been the disappointing outcome of more than one friendship that at one point appeared to be full of promise. It has equally been the cause of regret that the futures that beckoned and claimed us have led us in different directions, and the bonds of friendship have not been strong enough to survive.

Nevertheless, the joy of friendship remains and persists as one of the great joys of my life. It *is* possible, despite what Adams claimed, to be gifted through many friendships, each unique in its own particular shape, none of them diminished by the separation of distance or the passage of time. Upon reuniting, it is not necessary to retrace our steps, or to lay the foundation again. We rejoice in the meeting, and go on.

When Blanche Edwards Mesley, a sister to F. Henry Edwards and wife to the Australian apostle, died in 1990, my friend Paul wrote a moving tribute for the Australian *Saints Herald*. In summing up the life of this gracious stalwart of the church, Paul wrote: "She banked her treasure in the hearts of her friends, and there it will stay till their time is come." I would wish to say the same of my friends, in whom I have found a great treasure.

The Quilt of Friendship
By Joann and Clayton Condit

"Friendship is a golden cord," it has been said, or "True friends are like pearls along our line of life." We murmur noncommittally but our inner thoughts shout, "Not *our* friends!" In our experience, true friendship is not a golden cord to bind us but serves, rather, to free us. Our friends are not uniformly sized, "just exactly alike" pearls—no indeed. Although very precious, each one is unique, special, different. Our friends are more like a lovely old patchwork quilt.

Quilts come in all colors, and the best ones, in our eyes, present a splash of color like a kaleidoscope, a burst of joy. We have friends of many colors and each one is a deep joy to the center of our being. A quick glance over the quilt of our lives and we see all colors and shades, and we smile in joyful appreciation of how they all have melded together in that special gift from God called *friends*.

Quilts are made up of many shapes: blocks, triangles, diamonds, strips thin and strips wide. Pieced together, they form unique patterns of great beauty. In that same way, our quilt of friends shows us the beauty of many different personalities and peoples. There are those who are gentle, or some perhaps a little different. There are those who comfort and sustain, as well as those who need comforting and a shoulder on which to cry. There are friends who are quiet and peaceable and others who inspire us to giddy laughter. There are strong friends whose confiding handclasps or warm hugs bring joy far greater than they can know. There are elderly friends who surprise us with the wealth of life they have accumulated—and the youthful twinkle in their eyes. There are those of similar age, temperament, and experience—all shapes, all sizes, all colors, all personalities, all ages, all friends. And oh, the joy they bring.

The rescued scraps of fabric inspire us to delighted remembrance. "Oh, look at this one! I remember that dress.... I wore it to start the third grade!" "Oh my, I haven't thought of those pajamas for years and years, I loved that material!" With awe, "Mom, is this piece *actually* from one of Granny's dresses? *Truly*!" What a privilege and a blessing it is to be with friends and recall and rejoice over shared memories, the disappointments and sorrows, the jokes and puns, and all the amusing pieces that make up the fabric of our friendship.

Mixed in among all the colors and patterns of a quilt one finds small flashes of color that draw the eye and warm the heart, colors so vibrant that our eyes are drawn again and again to that particular color, that particular pattern. Too few of those exotic colors or textures and our quilt is somewhat lacking. It is a well-made quilt, a strong quilt, but it is, quite frankly, dull. Too many splashes of peacock and purple, green and gold, and we are overwhelmed; our minds cannot encompass what our vision insists is true. Mixed in among the friends of our lifetimes are those rare ones who seem to shimmer with charm, with excitement, with intelligence. We are enchanted, stimulated to accept new concepts, new learning. We stretch and grow and find enormous joy in our association. No less precious are the dear people who move in and through our lives quietly, peaceably, restfully. They are a solid foundation, a constant strength, and pure, quiet contentment.

Quilts endure. Quilts are passed down from generation to generation. Quilts get themselves displayed in such places as the Smithsonian. Those fragments of fabric may fade perhaps, or some of the stitches give way. Sometimes the fabric actually shreds, from age or ill usage. However, carefully tended, with delicate and invisible stitches, the quilt endures. True friendship endures as well. Sometimes we must tend the small rips and lost stitches, but like the quilt, a mended friendship emerges stronger than ever, and continues to endure. This shared saving of our entwined lives is joy, doubled and redoubled.

Quilts are made up of many patterns, many designs, all employing those small scraps of otherwise useless fabric. The designs of quilts most often arise out of the experiences of people in times of joy and triumph, or times of sorrow and pain. These keen emotions have been built into the pattern of the quilt itself, the sentiments and patterns transmuted from heart to a tangible template of the storms and victories of life. In our deepest associations with others, we share our grief, our remorse, and the multiple mishaps of life. In that same way, we share our elation, our delight, the large and small incidents that make up our lives. What a joy it is to find those whose spirits mesh with our own to form a unique and remarkable pattern.

Quilts are assembled with an inner core that insulates and retains warmth, a sturdy backing that will endure for many years, and a carefully assembled top that displays the chosen pattern. It is not a single entity, but comprises several levels. Just so does true friendship reach far beyond mere acquaintance. At its core is warmth and comfort. It wraps us about with security. The backing of friendship is sturdy and does not stretch out of shape. The glorious top layer may "travel" in as many directions as the crafted designs of geometric shapes, swoops, and whorls may indicate, but the patterns always turn and repeat.

May we give thanks for the friendships stitched firmly into our own fabric of life, for the comfort and warmth, beauty and remembrance, they provide to us daily. They are to be treasured and cherished, accepted as a blessing, a comfort, a special gift in our lives. If we might be allowed to paraphrase: *"Friendship! A thing of beauty and a joy forever!"*

What Are Friends For?
By Frank Kelley

Beside our need for a meaning, also a need for human intimacy without conventional trappings—for the experience of a circle where power expresses itself in meaningful and beautiful forms.[3]

A man I worked with used to ask, with only a fraction of his tongue in his cheek, "What are friends for, if you can't take advantage of them?" Through the years, I have reflected on this morsel of cynical humor. My conclusion: there are identifiable categories of people in our life's experience. And, it seems, we have different assumptions and expectations for each group. These categories range over a wide spectrum of relationships and encounters. To discuss friendship requires some definition—that is, some observations that differentiate that category of persons from all others.

We all know there are situations that require a certain impression to be made. This may involve a number of circumstances—a job interview, a court appearance, and, of course, anything involving a chance for romance. T. S. Eliot saw keenly that we have a need to feel secure about how we appear, and wrote:

Here will be time, there will be time
To prepare a face to meet the faces that you meet.[4]

Friendship does not depend on the faces we may or not have prepared. Friends are in the special category of individuals who know us as individuals, and choose to like us anyway.

Decades ago my wife and I were invited to a dinner party. About a dozen of us sat around the table over coffee, visiting. The hostess noted my admiration of some truly fine crystal in a cabinet nearby. She blossomed as she told me from whence it had come, from whom, and for what great occasion. "We only use it," she gushed, "for special guests."

Friends belong to that unique category of persons for whom each is always and at all times a "special guest." Friends come to our home, and my wife is eager to do and use our very best on their behalf, honoring them with warm regard. At the same time, deep inside, we sense that we could serve or be served a drink of water in a tin can and the relationship would lose nothing at all. Friendship does not depend on props for sustenance. Just being together— or thinking about being together—does unique things to friends, as John Ciardi explained:

Like old faces
Being fed a good memory
from inside themselves.[5]

As I slide rapidly toward my seventh decade, memories of this and that surface at odd moments in a variety of locations—a kind of mental swamp gas: thoughts, ideas, and fragments produced by the mixture of who knows what, deep in the rolling mind. One such bubble burst recently, revealing a phrase from a Beatles' song— "What you see in me!" Friends are members of that category of humanity, your relationship with whom, not propped up by superficial impression and artifice, is fueled simply by who and what you are—and most importantly, who and what you are when you are together. Being with a friend is akin to gazing into a mirror and seeing someone else gaze back, someone you recognize with surprise and joy, as more of yourself than you knew existed.

Kahlil Gibran, a popular poet often cranked up at weddings and funerals, unfortunately, but uniquely gifted with a blend of profound insight and perfectly faceted phrase, sensed the special quality of friendship and described it thus:

Your friend is your needs answered,
He is your field which you sow with love and reap with
thanksgiving.
And he is your board and your fireside.
For you come to him with your hunger, and you seek him for
peace.[6]

If there is a downside to all this—and we know there must be an opposition in all things—it is that for most of us, the people we can truly identify as friends is such a small cadre. I, like you, treasure these chosen ones, these special persons, for whom we are simply ourselves without fear, and with whom the relationship is its own reason for being. By striking coincidence, I ran across a piece of verse by Barbara Gibbs, reflecting on the Beatles' aforementioned popular ditty:

> **But we know that it's**
> **Impossible**
> **If what the song says were true**
> **And we could all open our eyes at once**
> **And see one another**
> **Right then we'd be in heaven.**[7]

And we'd all be friends.

Notes

1. Alexander Pope, letter to Jonathan Swift (December 5, 1732).
2. Henry Brooks Adams, in *The Education of Henry Adams* (1907).
3. Dag Hammarskjöld, *Markings* (New York: Alfred A. Knopf, 1977), 4.
4. T. S. Eliot, *The Waste Land* (New York: Harvest Books, 1962), 4.
5. John Ciardi, "Returning Home," *Poems of Love and Marriage* (Fayetteville, Arkansas: University of Arkansas Press, 1988), 5.
6. Kahlil Gibran, *The Prophet* (New York: Alfred A. Knopf, 1964), 58.
7. Barbara Gibbs, "What You See in Me," *The New Yorker Book of Poems* (New York: The Viking Press, 1969), 805.

Chapter 8

The  of Remembrance

Thanks for the Memories
By Frank Kelley

Frequently and with deliberation and respect we should revisit our early memories—memories which do not fade which hold the incorruptible essence of emotion.[1]

An old and yellowed clipping from a long-forgotten Sunday comic strip ("Pickles," by Brian Cane) tells the story of our aged hero declaring to his curious daughter his reasons for feeling that he is "a very lucky man." He concludes, "I have lived a long and very full life, and yet I am able to look back with contentment and a complete sense of serenity. Do you know why that is? Because I have a very poor memory."

Remembering is what we do with that very special faculty we call memory. Remembering is the process of *recollection*—the bringing together again of the senses, impressions, and often scattered elements of a particular experience or pieces of information. To remember is literally to *re-member*—to once more construct a bit of personal history from the bits of data and perceptions tucked away in the labyrinth that is our mind.

The faculty of memory can be experienced as a two-edged sword. I remember well how I looked and felt as a young marine: fit, energized, equipped with all the necessary drive and appropriate hormonal power. Now longer in tooth, I share Robert W. Smith's psalm, "Thank God mirrors don't have memories."[2] Others have also lamented the baggage represented by the passing of years and the accompanying revival of experience.

E. M. Cioran looks back with longing and wishes things had been otherwise. "Our disease?" he cries. "Centuries of attention to time, the idolatry of becoming."[3] Peter heard that fateful cock crow, and wept bitterly.

On balance, however, the capacity for remembrance is a marvelous gift. Bronstein writes;

> **… in the halls of memory copies of the vivid impressions of the moment are stored up. From these I draw each one out as I wish. But the copy is not transitory like the sensation it mirrors; it has a continued existence. It is the same as, yet different from the sensation. The past is preserved as it was, yet it is intrinsically different.**[4]

A memory is a wonderful composite of experience, selectivity, sensation, reflection, and judgment. One day, when I was about ten years or so of age, I was working on schoolwork (an actual experience), the nature of which is now lost to me (selectivity), on a blackboard my father had installed on the east wall of our kitchen. Hank, a friend of my future sister-in-law, came into the room, engaged me in conversation, and explained the problem I was attempting to solve or understand. The explanation was accompanied by a physical experience (sensation) that I could not then describe or comprehend. Years later in a college English class, the professor stated that encounters with significant truth can be "like the opening up of the top of one's head." This is as close to a description of the boy in the kitchen at the blackboard as I have found. The passage of time and the accumulation of life's experiences have allowed me to reflect on that episode and make a judgment as to its significance. I have since had many experiences in various circumstances in which the top of my head was opened. I recognize that sensation as an important aspect of my encounter with the transcendent. This simple happening—the coming together of Hank, the problem, the blackboard, and myself—occurred more than fifty years ago. The recounting of it has involved an infinite number of mental, physical, and spiritual impressions and reflections.

So Jesus, on that memorable evening, celebrating that special observance, in that sacred place with those select associates, shared bread and wine—the most common of elements—and instructed them to do it *in remembrance* of him (Matthew 26). I can barely imagine what their memories must have stored away about that supper. As time passed, and with it experiences and understandings and the inevitable metamorphoses of the spirit—what words could suffice? And for us as well, so far removed from all that; our memories are firsthand of experience and meaning passed and filtered through those of countless generations since. How shall we muster the enormous, amazing power of memory in the face or encounters with the holy?

I read a story once about a man who had a strange affliction. When he slept each night, his memory bank was completely erased. He awoke each morning knowing nothing of his past. He started each day with an absolutely blank slate. I can imagine few things more frightening. Death would be preferable to such a grotesque "living." Knowing that I am gifted with memory—a fallible capacity as those close to me know only too well—I am faced with the task of choosing what I shall remember. It is a choice that becomes more demanding.

I don't want to remember everything. Every so often I cull my files and desk drawers of papers, quotes, articles, and such. Computer programs are available to remove redundancies and unused files. I must ask myself *why* a particular journal or book should be saved. Culling books is the "Gethsemane" of an avid reader. A good friend suggested that I acquire no more books until I had read—completely—every book I now possess. I may have to consider culling good friends.

If I am to take Christianity seriously, I am faced with the same daunting task. What shall I choose to remember? What is the complex of my experience, sensation, reflection, and judgment telling me I need in order to be equipped to be a disciple of the Lord Jesus? What, in the final analysis, is vital, and what can be—like the files and drawers and computer drives—simply culled? Even in this— perhaps one of the most significant choices of one's life—memory is a key element. I must rely, for my primary source, on others recalling what Jesus said and did. Those memories tell a story of a time when Jesus himself was faced with that issue. He is reported to have said there are two things first of all worth remembering: love God with everything available to you—your heart, mind, soul, and strength; and love your neighbor as yourself. I choose to remember these things. I am convinced they shall suffice.

Sam Keen struggled with all of this and came to a conclusion: "We age in order to become lovers."[5] That's worth remembering.

A Storehouse of Remembrances
By Don and Helen Lents

From the perspective of a lifetime of service to the church, Don and Helen Lents recall people and events that have enriched their lives:

The gift of remembrance is like a patchwork quilt: pieces of assorted colors, varied shapes, differing types of fabric created into a meaningful and beautiful pattern. Our treasured gems of joyful remembrances fit together in a similar way

We think of our families: parents Victor and Delia Lents, Earl and Olive Draper, whose trust in the Lord and love for their children introduced us to extended families of our congregations in Rhodes, Iowa, and San Bernardino, California.

A little gem of a wheelchair-bound woman named Mattie Hughes testified of good men and women, both of scriptures and the current day, bringing to life appreciation for and knowledge of scriptures and life well lived. She also issued the first invitation to Roy A. Cheville to "come to church and see" in the Rhodes congregation. A number of years later, in 1943, he officiated at our marriage.

A dearly loved teacher of children, Eva Goff, guided those of the San Bernardino congregation in activities of the church's Religio program, making our faith journey exciting and adventuresome activities. Religious drama under the direction of Irene Stearns in that same congregation modeled the lessons of scripture and Christian discipleship.

Mentors who saw possibilities in emerging talents and skills brought encouragement and confidence, creating opportunities for participation in expanding experiences of reunions and district activities of the Des Moines and Southern California Districts during our teen years. Names such as Henry Castings, Clyde McDonald, and Ormond Salisbury come to mind among those who saw something in a young man who sometimes made it difficult for them to mentor him.

After the early death of Earl Draper the support of others for the five Draper children was a very important part of the spiritual development of the family. James (Jimmy) Burdick, Bishop David Carmichael, Glaude A. Smith, Josie Lee and Dick Hacker, Mayme Blakeman, George and Lola Scott, and Hunter Ferguson are remembered with fondness for their love and caring friendship.

The stirring of a sense of call was supported by stalwarts of the church, stimulating an affirmative response to a two-year (which became four years) appointee who needed knowledge and guidance in his emerging ministerial service. Important assistance was generously shared by Apostles John Garver, George Lewis, F. Henry Edwards, Blair Jensen, and others. Roscoe and Mabel Davey (Maw and Paw Davey) became mentors for a young, inexperienced couple desiring to serve the people of the church. Their devotion and positive attitude was exemplary as we charted our own paths of service and commitment.

Those who nurtured our children as they learned to love the Lord hold a special place in our hearts: Agnes Edmunds (church school teacher), Delmar and Charlotte Prine , DeLoyd and Iris Winship (Zion's League leaders), Don Stonger and Chester Kramer (Scout leaders) of West College congregation, and John and Marilyn Shank of East 39th St. congregation (Zioneer and Zion's League leaders). Bishop G. Leslie DeLapp was also a special mentor and valued friend.

In reflecting on the spirit of joy that has permeated our remembrances, we are overwhelmed by a feeling of gratitude for the many places and people who have blessed our lives. The experiences of worshiping in Europe with a diverse group in unity of spirit who were just a few years removed from being "enemies at war" with one another, the support of kind, trustworthy men such as John Coggan, Edgar Holmes, John Worth, and Franklyn Schofield in the British Isles; the encouragement of women such as Gertrude

Allen and Elva Oakman who helped draw forth ministries that were part of the preparation for priesthood calls to women—these readily come to mind. The warmth of hospitality, and the prayers and actions of caring during needy times for our families—all these are part of the fabric of remembrances of joy. Wealth is counted not in things, but in relationships such as the fellowship of the Saints, and we are wealthy indeed.

Poised between Past and Future
By Geoff Spencer

> *O remember*
> *In your narrowing dark hours*
> *That more things move*
> *Than blood in the heart.*[6]

Although this citation from Louise Bogan may appear somewhat morbid, it is nevertheless true that the passsage of time brings with it an enlivening of the memory. It seems to me that there are many times when the vivid recollections of past events, people, situations, and feelings are so strong that they take on a life of their own within us and propel us into the present moment as surely as the blood that flows in our veins.

This is not to suggest that we are most alive when we exist in a kind of captivating nostalgia, yearning for the "good old days" (or *daze*, as my cynical father would sometimes have rendered it), but that the accumulated experiences of the past shape, in a very positive way, the framework out of which we perceive, evaluate, decide, and act in a profoundly important way.

In this chapter I have substantially reproduced what I wrote in an earlier publication.[7] I want to reaffirm the observations I shared then in describing the church as a remembering community, except that I do so now with a depth and intensity that I do not think was possible almost two decades ago. More than ever I see no exaggeration in the assertion that we are what we remember. The power to remember is fundamental to human personhood and identity. We are, in fact, shaped by what we remember, consciously or unconsciously. Without a memory we can hardly be a self, either an individual or a communal self.

Memory is more than a luxury for those who choose to wallow in the past. It is the lively, imaginative, and organizing activity that permits us to live in the world with a sense of identity and coherence. Sundered from memory, each one of us will ask, in fear and trembling, the first question that automatically erupts from the amnesiac's sense of lostness: "Who am I?" I remember, with infinitely more understanding now than then, the terror in a dear friend's plea when I visited him in an institution for the emotionally disturbed, as he searched in vain for some clue to his identity. My natural response was to try to bring to the surface experiences we had shared, until I had to accept the fact the past was a closed door to him.

On April 25 each year, the great majority of Australians and New Zealanders pause to recall the occasion in 1915 when troops from those two countries took part in an assault on the beaches of Gallipoli on the Turkish peninsula. The venture, ill-conceived and premature, culminated in a defeat for the attack force that has been described as "a tragic blunder and heroic failure." Yet the events have been preserved in the memory of subsequent generations as a symbolic witness to the courage and endurance that, by report, were exhibited in the Gallipoli landing. The time came when I conducted the funeral service for two of my uncles who had been part of that campaign. The story was very real to me.

Obviously, to say that something is important is to imply, "Important for whom?" Our meanings, values, and priorities are shaped by the memories evoked in the shared experience of the communities of which we are a part. For us, the community of the church is the guardian of those memories and is sustained through time and space by the memories it lifts up. Some time ago, one of our sons, as a young newspaper reporter for the *Independence Examiner,* was assigned to cover World Conference. Having grown up in a church home, he was reasonably well acquainted with the vocabulary and references that abound in our communications. Nevertheless, much escaped him, sometimes nothing more than a subtle nuance, a passing reference, an allusion in our RLDS-ese. A fellow reporter from the *Kansas City Times* was completely mystified much of the time. Even when the words, taken separately, were familiar, there was no connectedness or coherence without memory.

Some years ago, two Christian educators leveled criticism at what they called "the forgetful society," claiming that our contemporary technological society suffers from a kind of collective amnesia. Such a deprivation was, they believed, not only unfortunate but tragic in its consequences.

It was been suggested that the meaninglessness in life in contemporary America, its frequent banality, results from the sterility of conscious community memory…. Outside the private home there is very little that feeds the memory, and within it, unless we make a consistent effort, it rapidly falls away. How can God disclose himself to a people who have no way to speak of his presence, who are culturally retarded? Even more, what is the possibility of our seeing God if our memories are barren?[8]

It bears repeating that in the conscious memory of the community are the resources that provide the meaning for that community and its sense of direction for the future. The roots of the church are not so much traced to a series of good ideas and moral principles but to concrete events in which God was believed to have been present and active.

To ascribe such a vital role to memory, however, is not to suggest that memory should be undisciplined. People might find "joy" in nostalgia or in fantasy, which is selective or imaginative memory. There is a clear and important distinction between dwelling in the past, wishing that our memories could be magically restored in our own day, and living out of the past, so that a vital and contemporary response is informed and energized by a sense of what has gone before.

The past is peculiarly vulnerable to distortion, because it is not able to defend itself, so to speak. It is all too easy for individuals or groups to manipulate what has gone before to construct a creature of fantasy, serving personal or institutional ends. It is not necessary to construct major works of falsification, monuments of deception. The evidence is abundant that there is no more insidious way to revise the past than by "slight retouches, displacements, discolorations, omission, shifts of accent."[9]

Faithfulness is therefore at the mercy of memory. By intent or by accident, memory can function as an accessory both to fact and figment. When Abraham Lincoln gave his first inaugural address at a time of great crisis, he indicated that he was prepared to use force if necessary to preserve the Union, but placed his confidence in a much more persuasive force. "The mystic chords of memory," he asserted, "will yet swell the chorus of the Union."[10] At the same time, the new president did not see memory as a free-floating grace released from accountability. Rather, memory needed to be touched "by the better angels of our nature," responsive to the demands of integrity.

As a young boy I sometimes spent vacations at the home of one of my aunts. Her youngest son, considerably older than I, was a prominent football player, renowned for his toughness and strength. He was a veritable giant, and so I remembered him in the years that followed, when I lost contact with him. Then we met again, and I was astonished to find that he was no giant, but actually shorter than I. Memory had created a figure that simply didn't exist—innocent enough, in all probability, and perhaps even to be expected as a young child's recollections. Yet individuals, families, or groups, and especially nations, have cultivated their myths for reasons that do not stand close scrutiny. Latter Day Saints have sometimes been so intent on establishing an organizational identity with the primitive Jerusalem community that there has emerged, mentally, a New Testament church that never actually existed as we remembered it.

There may be temporary satisfaction, but there is no lasting joy if memory fails to exhibit honesty, and the dispelling of the "myths" may be extremely painful. In a statement that is, for me, profoundly moving, David Baily Harned has written:

The rectitude of memory is priceless; without it we lose touch with ourselves and with the narrative of our lives. Then, too, the shared memories of our communities afford the only lodging there is for the great stories that inform and grant significance to the small narrative of the individual. If memory plays false with us, the stories are twisted and diminished, and by that much are our possibilities of action curtailed.[11]

As members of the church, we find ourselves blessed to be part of a community that honors and nourishes our personal memories as well as those of the corporate body. The church's memories are preserved and celebrated in the stories, dramas, and rituals that link past and present in a dynamic relationship. Further, our personal memories are affirmed and celebrated in the context of the larger community that reaches backward in time and outward in space far beyond our individual capacity. Is it any wonder that the faithful of another time could confess, "If I forget thee, O Jerusalem, let my right hand forget its cunning. If I do not remember thee, let my tongue cleave to the roof of my mouth" (Psalm 137:5–6).

The memories of the church can be brought to life and nurtured in the lives of our families. I was once visiting in the homes of church member friends who, as part of a family celebration, took a china cup and saucer from the sideboard, smashed them into pieces and then mixed the pieces in with plaster to form a symbolic object. They were reminding themselves and their children that members of the church in an earlier day had similarly offered their tableware and ornaments to enhance the walls of Kirtland Temple. In so doing they were dramatically acknowledging a debt to the predecessors and identifying themselves as part of the one body continuing through time, bonded by common memories and commitments.

Granting all that has been said about the function of memory, there is yet a dimension to the church's remembering—and to that of each one of us— that is highly significant. To *dis*-member is to separate the constituent parts of some entity that is essentially one. To *re*-member is to bring those parts back into a living relationship. Thus, for the church, remembering is the vital process of regeneration by which the life of Christ is continually recreated in the midst of the community. Divided and separated within ourselves, and from others, we find the walls of separation and dismemberment broken down, and the community brought to healing and wholeness.

What a joy it is to remember!

Notes

1. Robert Grudin, *Time and the Art of Living* (New York: Ticknor & Fields, 1981), 172.
2. Robert W. Smith, cited in James L. Christian, *Philosophy: An Introduction to Wondering,* Fourth edition (New York: Holt, Rinehart and Winston, 1996), 148.
3. E. M. Cioran, *The Temptation to Exist* (London: Ouartet Books, 1987), 35.
4. Daniel J. Bronstein, Phillip P. Wiener, and Yervant H. Krikorian, eds. *Basic Problems of Philosophy* (Englewood Cliffs, New Jersey: Prentice-Hall, 1972), 43.
5. Sam Keen, *The Passionate Life* (San Francisco: Harper Collins, 1984), 30.
6. Louise Bogan (1897–1970).
7. *Strangers and Pilgrims: Images of the Church for Today* (Herald House, 1984).
8. Urban T. Holmes and John W. Westerhoff III, *Christian Believing* (New York: The Seabury Press, 1979), 80.
9. Joseph Pieper, *The Four Cardinal Values* (New York: Harcourt Brace Jovanovich, 1965), 21.
10. Abraham Lincoln, "First Inaugural Address" (March 4, 1861).
11. David Baily Harned, *Faith and Virtue* (Philadelphia: Pilgrim Press, 1973), 177.

Chapter 9

The  of Teaching/Learning

And Gladly Wolde He Lerne, and Gladly Teche. [1]
By Geoff Spencer

If there is any book in my library that might conceivably qualify as a "rare volume" it is the first edition (1938) of the *Commentary on the Doctrine and Covenants* by F. Henry Edwards. I have ascertained that the Temple library does not possess a copy, and it is just possible that someday I might (in a moment of weakness) donate the book to their holdings.

The frontispiece to this volume carries the inscription: "To Geoffrey Spencer, Special Prize, Campsie Church School, 1942." I had just turned fifteen. The pastor had decided I had served as a deacon long enough to learn the basic duties associated with the care of the building and believed I should be introduced to some of the broader aspects of my calling. As he pondered the calling of the deacon (in assisting the teacher) to "warn, expound, exhort, and teach," he concluded, I suspect, that the ministry of teaching would best (and perhaps most safely) fall within the scope of a young man of my tender years, a ministry in which I could inflict the least damage. Accordingly he arranged for me to be given the Edwards text with the announcement that I would be using this text to teach the adult class, beginning the following February.

It ruined Christmas for me!

But in the midst of that painful and demanding venture I experienced the first hints of a respect and passion for teaching that has stayed with me ever since; through my qualification as a professional schoolteacher, my years of practicing my profession until I became a World Church appointee minister in 1954, and ever thereafter. The same has been true of learning, for certainly in that initial experience I learned more about the Doctrine and Covenants than the members of the class, who were in reality my teachers. Indeed, I have come to understand the truth of the adage that "to teach is to learn twice."

I must confess there was a time when my curiosity and passion for learning encountered head-on a stubborn resistance that was part of my religious heritage. I had heard many times quoting Doctrine and Covenants 43:46 that, as members of the Restoration, we were "not sent forth to be taught, but to teach" (a "truth" impressed on me in that first teaching experience) even if sometimes we appeared to be giving answers to questions that people were no longer asking, or had never asked. And so, whenever I might be faced with the terror and uncertainty of encountering new understandings that had the potential to expand my horizons, I adopted the simple expediency of closing my ears to what I was hearing, or my eyes to what I was reading.

At the same time, some inner voice repeatedly told me I was adopting a short-sighted response to new ideas and that my curiosity would get the better of my stubborn blindness. I remember with deep affection one friend in my congregation, an elder by the name of Andrew Waugh. The pastor had asked me and another young deacon, Gordon McLaughlin, to share our first preaching service, and so at the age of fourteen I took ten minutes to tell the congregation everything I "knew"—twice. For reasons that may be obvious, members of the congregation were delighted at the offering of these two young men, and highly complimentary in their remarks. Imagine my unease when Andy, as I came to know him, an elder of mature years, said, "Geoff, there are just one or two points I wasn't clear on about what you said. Perhaps we could talk about these some time." When I shared my discomfort with my mother she was wise enough to suggest that rather than expecting compliments, I should be grateful to Andy who was willing to treat me as an adult, worthy of mature conversation and mature learning.

On the last occasion I saw Andy, visiting him in a nursing home during one of my periodic visits home to Australia, he made the same observation. Although blind and unable to pursue his beloved reading, he had listened while his daughter read from my latest book and had "one or two points that weren't too clear" that he wished to discuss with me.

I will always be grateful for good friends such as Andy and for the counsel of my parents, as well as for my own basic impulse. I grew to love the adventure and to absorb the threat of new ideas in the joy of discovery. And always, in the very act of teaching, I find myself once again a learner. Indeed, it is often true that I do not know precisely what I am thinking until I hear myself saying it, as if a source from outside my conscious self had entered the dialogue and was prompting the course to take. What is true is that wherever I find myself at any moment in the teaching/learning spectrum, it is a continuing joy and challenge.

In the statements that follow, we share the testimonies of two individuals who exhibit the excitement of the teacher and the curiosity of the learner, and have been siezed by the wonder of the journey.

Born to Grow
By Daniel K. Sage

Something miraculous happens when people learn. They grow; they change. Their world grows; their world changes. The whole world grows and changes.

Watch people who are around a child who is just learning to walk or talk. The child's environment is alive with celebrations over small steps made and bumbled words spoken. Learning is happening. No one really "teaches" the infant how to walk or talk. The learning is essentially natural. Family and friends revel in the chance to join this process in whatever way possible. But everyone knows the learning transcends mere steps and mere words. Even the infant, to a very large degree, is only a participant-observer in this miracle. The forces of life are in control.

We are born to grow. Growing and learning are the most human form of realities in life. Teaching, at its best, creates conditions so that natural growth and learning can flourish. Of course, it is not without pain and hardship that we grow, nor without degrees of challenge and suffering that we learn. Yet teaching bears witness to the miracle in *all* growth and learning. Ultimately, teaching invites us to be more fully human, to discover more about ourselves and each other. Teaching glories in our humanity. Teaching celebrates life.

That is why I teach. That is why learning for me is a joy. In teaching I remain close to the pulse of the miracle of learning. Here I feel most alive. It is flattering to think that as a teacher I play some small role in the transforming experiences of learners. But it is delusional to believe that I bestow upon the learners something they do not already have.

Make no mistake. I do not always enjoy teaching. Teachers deal with concerns intimately connected to all potentials of the human condition. But in its wholeness teaching is a joy. The mysteries of teaching—really great teaching—are not quantifiable. Yet there is something about genuine teaching and authentic experiences of learning that are unmistakable. Learning manifests the miracle of growth, and teaching stakes claim to the wonder of the miracle. In the midst of the ordinary, the teacher finds the extraordinary.

In the final analysis, what life asks of us is to grow and to learn. How we choose to grow and learn determines the quality of our lives. We can live as if we are already dead, or we can live life to the fullest. Regardless of the terms on which life is offered to us, the choice is ours.

Teaching sides with those who choose to live life to the fullest. The entire enterprise of teaching, learning, and living becomes a seamless collaboration. The learner becomes the teacher and the teacher becomes the learner in the miracle of living. When real growth and learning are happening one can scarcely tell where learning begins and teaching leaves off. All titles and rankings become lost in a web of discoveries and linkings. Few human experiences can compare to such miracles. That is why I teach. What a joy!

The Passion to Be Involved
By Paul M. Edwards

*Two men look out through the prison bars
One sees mud—one sees stars.*[2]

It has been nearly forty years since I taught my first class and spoke, for the first time, before an audience. There must have been hundreds, if not thousands of occasions since that beginning. Yet I remember the first time with a clarity given to little else. I was so nervous I had trouble controlling myself. I checked and rechecked my notes. I glanced at my watch every thirty seconds. As I waited for the class to begin, I planned the opening sentence over and over again. I felt in my inner self a feeling like fear and like love, a very strange combination of pride and of humility. I was acutely aware that other minds were depending on me, that I was expected to know something, and that I owed them, in return for their time and presence, to provide something worthwhile.

During the period in which I was writing this short statement, my schedule called for me to teach two classes. Before each I was, as always, so nervous I had trouble containing myself. It was the same feeling. I have had this feeling before each such occasion ever since. Over the years, the aggravation has been fed by the growing realization of how smart people are and how much they invest in the issues I dared discuss. I have grown increasingly afraid they will be short-changed. "This is the time," that mean little voice whispers in my ear, "that they will discover just how little you know."

At these times I tend to forget everything I ever knew. But when it is over I try to take seriously Paul Tillich's comment that the neurotic is not the man or woman who is anxious, but the one who feels because of his or her anxiety cut off from the possibility of their own being by the fear of their exposure. The long evolution, or perhaps the sudden leap, from innocence to experience is found in this anxiety. And it is this experience that I define as joy. By joy I mean the sudden and prolonged feeling of being alive. It is different from happiness, which I tend to define as that state of not knowing you are unhappy. I am not without my dark side. People often interpret my tendency to realism as pessimism. But, with no attempt to be funny, I am very positive when you consider the shape the world is in. And while this dark side emerges, even in the wonderful anxiety of teaching, the more powerful and consistent condition is happiness.

Happiness, therefore, is to be defined as the sum that emerges from the swings in intensity reflected by joy, as well as by the sadness, of living one's life. For the sake of our hope, the sadness is not without its gift of personal awareness. For the sake of sanity, the joy is not without the stress of maintaining our own identity, a situation we identify as anxiety. Interestingly, it is the search for freedom from anxiety that renders us intensely subject to the very anxiety we are trying to escape. The source of one's anxiety is the passion of one's involvement, and it is the passion that provides the anxiety. Without the passion there is no anxiety, but there is also no happiness. The paradox is—and yes it is a paradox—that it is the passion to be involved that is both the source of, and the answer to, the alienation of humanity in this awesome age. For me this moment of paradox lies in successfully overcoming the strong feeling of separation without the elimination of others. For me the paradox is found in the work I do, which I pursue as an act of creation that allows me to be united with the society, without being dissolved in it, or by it.

Response to the paradox is defined by Martin Buber as "heart searching," by which he means the accomplishment of the unique demands people make on themselves. The more we love, the greater the passion, the higher the costs. The costs are found in the difficulty of trying to be both unique and communal: recognizing that what a person is cannot be understood without including what a person ought to be.

I am grateful beyond adequate expression for the joy of this anxiety. What I mean by this is that I am thankful for the anxiety created by the clash between a growing knowledge of who I am, and who I must be to assure some acceptance to and for my community. I am thankful for my uniqueness. I am thankful for the acknowledgment of my being, and for the opportunities to bring myself face to face with others. I am thankful for the chance to walk with the community, with the presence of nature, with knowledge, with wonder, and of God. And I am thankful to find those moments in which I am so aware of my being that I am almost out of control, and glance at my watch every thirty seconds, and both fear and love with great intensity at the same moment.

A Latter Day Saint's Love of Learning
By Frank Kelley

The delights of the mind are superior in quality to any other form of enjoyment. Intellectual acquisitions are, indeed, the only forms of wealth which once attained and used can never be lost—which do not lose their luster with time.[3]

I have enjoyed a love affair with school for well over fifty years. Among my many early memories are those of kindergarten in the lower level of the Central Park School. It was great sport, running in a noisy, barnlike room filled with other young primitives, stacking big blocks, and having my very own little quilt on which to nap. That quilt was homemade, warm, I recall, and flannel of some dark color, smelling comfortably of me and who can say what else. I know I did not like it when the authorities insisted it be washed, as it then became foreign and not right somehow. (So I understood well when our little terrier, Butch, objected if his box under the stove was cleaned and his bed or rags laundered. He didn't like that, either.)

You may ask appropriately why my reflection on learning is launched at such a childish level. What have noise, naps, and nonsense to do with the life of the mind—that capacity that more than any other sets us apart from most of God's creation? I must confess that for me, the business of learning, schooling, and teaching are at base sensual matters. I love the feel of books, the smell of chalk, and the peculiar, indefinable atmosphere of electric anticipation of people—young and old—gathered to learn, teach, and expand: in short, those who come together to become more than they presently are. True learning, for me, has always engaged the corporeal as well as the intellectual faculties.

We of the Restoration movement have long been learners. Joseph Smith Jr. established the School of the Prophets upstairs in the Kirtland Temple. The early Saints busily built schools wherever they went. Latter-day scriptures, from the earliest times, are consistent in exhorting us to learn and to grow in and through the learning process. In this, our movement participated in a trend of historical import. We were a vanguard in America in an institutional emphasis that was not only rooted in our response to our mission but to what Elias and Merriam refer to as "proposed new ways of seeking knowledge. Reason, experience and feeling began to replace tradition and authority as the chief ways of arriving at truth."[4] This trend had been in part stimulated by the growth in Europe of what came to be called "progressive" education, with a thrust of rationalistic, empirical, and scientific thought. As a people we have long been urged to find ourselves "in the forefront." And so it is entirely to be expected that we should learn that our souls are a wonderful blend of spirit and element, that our learning be a process not confined to our heads but involve our hearts and hands as well, and that all of this be only a part of a much greater thrust of the divine purpose on earth.

Another great thing about learning as a Latter Day Saint is the understanding that truth is where you find it, "independent in that sphere in which God has placed it" (Doctrine and Covenants 90:5b). Turning to the early instructions to the church (see Sections 85 and 87) the Saints were specifically directed to "seek learning by study and also by faith" and search "all good books" to know "languages, tongues, and people." And further, just in case this principle might be lost in the quagmire of differing experience and interpretation, we were advised to apply "in principle" those instructions already received (Doctrine and Covenants 147:7) and again, in 1968 (Doctrine and Covenants 149:5) we were reminded of the importance of "seeking more light and truth from all available sources." A friend once related that her husband viewed this approach to enlightenment, learning, and comprehension with disdain, as "religion a la carte—just believe what you want to believe and when." But I find this incredibly liberating and have sensed the Holy Presence in the writings and contemplations of many marvelous minds from diverse traditions.

Learning as a Latter Day Saint serves as a great source of joy for another reason very meaningful to me. I have met many unique and wonderful people who, along with us, are seeking. I am not speaking just about people who are schooled learners, with titles and degrees. Not all learning is specifically connected with, nor dependent on, formal education. Through the years, everywhere we have lived, I have encountered such people—members of a kind of underground society—for whom learning and knowing and stretching is a vital part of living. Because of the open stance of our movement, we are blessed to have these among us.

If there is a downside to the learning curve, it is that we live in a time that is witnessing an explosion of information and knowledge unparalleled in history. There is a bewildering array of fact and hypothesis confronting us on every hand. Our anchor in the currents of the lure to become more than we are, to extend the boundaries of our small selves, is the realization that we are a curious amalgam of mind and body, spirit and element. What we would learn and know somehow needs to be understood in already familiar terms—with what we have already perceived as true—in order for it to "fit" or be understood.

Arthur Koestler said it this way:

Absolutes are too inhuman and elusive to deal with, unless they are connected with some experience in the tangible world of the finite. In fact, eternity is a pretty meaningless notion—unless it is made to look through the window of time. "Immensity" is a bore….The absolute becomes emotionally effective only if it is associated with something concrete—dovetailed, as it were, into the familiar.[5]

I suspect that the force behind the divine directions and guidance we have received to be busy about the business of learning, and the tide within myself on which I am carried along, has its origins in that circumstance so aptly described by Koestler. We are tempted upward to and pulled into a process of apprehending those things which we have neither seen nor heard, nor that have entered our hearts (see I Corinthians 2) through our experiences and understanding of what is the familiar and the tangible. We are acquainted with this approach to learning through Jesus' parables. We are confronted by the validity of this method of comprehension of transcendent truth through Jesus' life and ministry. Theologians call this process *incarnation*. It is to this same end that we as Latter Day Saints are called to learn, and why.

Notes

1. Geoffrey Chaucer, Prologue to *The Canterbury Tales* (c 1386).
2. Frederick Langbridge, as found in *A Cluster of Quiet Thoughts* (Religious Tract Society, 1886).
3. Eduard Lindeman C., *The Meaning of Adult Education* (Norman, Oklahoma: University of Oklahoma, 1986), xxvi.
4. John L. Elias and Sharan Merriam, *Philosophical Foundations of Adult Education* (Malabar, Florida: Robert E. Kreiger Publishing Co.), 46.
5. Arthur Koestler, *The Act of Creation* (New York: The MacMillan Co.), 364.

Chapter 10

Interlude: The Oil of Joy for Mourning

To this point we have shared convictions about several dimensions of living in which joy is available to us: a choice, albeit a gift. In most cases, the promise and prospect of joy is within view at the earliest stage, perhaps even from the beginning. Yet there are experiences in life that must be "lived through," times when joy might seem remote and beyond reach. Even in such matters as forgiveness and repentance, while there may be some strong disciplines called for, the outcomes are always within view, worthy of our best efforts.

Does this mean that joy is exclusively a fair-weather phenomenon, a valued companion for the brighter experiences and achievements of our lives, but abandoning us when the dark side confronts us—pain, sorrow, loss, grief—as inevitably it will? Can we really know the oil of joy for mourning, or is it an empty promise held out to people crushed under the burdens that can come so suddenly upon us, or haunt us as a long-term fear? (See Isaiah 63:1 and Luke 4:17–21.) It was this same Old Testament prophet whom Jesus chose to quote when handed the scroll during his visit to the synagogue in Nazareth, including the commitment to "heal the brokenhearted." The Lord deliberately found the place from which to read, and in so doing announced the nature of his own ministry. It bears our careful scrutiny.

At first sight it might seem that Lewis Smedes's claim that "only the heart that hurts has right to joy" is prompted by an oversized pessimism or a refusal to face facts—or life—honestly.[1] With the exception of those who are so tender in years they may not have yet encountered the "dark side," we have yet to meet another person whose entire life has been characterized by uninterrupted serenity. Nevertheless, in the final analysis, it will be the testimony of those who *have* experienced the dark side—and perhaps your own voice speaking to you—that gives assurance there can indeed be "a garment of splendor for the heavy heart" (Isaiah 61:3 NEB). Moreover, although we may be familiar with scriptural references or reasoned arguments upholding joy in such circumstances, it will be our lived out, even "suffered-through" experiences that carry the undeniable truth.

After ten years of living with continuous physical pain, the result of a mountain-climbing accident, Tim Hansel shared his encounter with joy in a book titled *You Gotta Keep Dancin'*. The author no doubt was speaking on behalf of many people who had passed through "the valley of the shadow," or were still struggling with the threat to stability and peace:

> **This book is in no way meant to diminish the awfulness of pain, tragedy, and affliction. I don't want to "celebrate pain," but more deeply understand the dignity of what can happen in it, through it, and because of it.[2]**

Some have claimed the apostle Paul wrote II Corinthians while in prison, though the weight of evidence appears to be against it. However, it is most likely that, in prison or not, Paul would still have described his own life, and that of his fellow believers, as "sorrowful, yet always rejoicing" (II Corinthians 6:10).

The following chapter invites you to share the journey of one of the authors of this book who, together with his companion, has emerged from a potentially crippling experience of loss and grief and yet lives with a compelling presence of joy. This is followed by two chapters in which loss and grief are explored separately, if indeed such is possible, and offer testimonies of those who speak from the heart.

Notes

1. Lewis B. Smedes, *How Can it Be All Right When Everything Is All Wrong* (New York: Harper & Row, 1982), 15.
2. Tim Hansel, *You Gotta Keep Dancin'* (Colorado Springs, Colorado: Cook Communications, 1985), 17.

Chapter 11

Still Waters in the Valley of the Shadow

By Frank Kelley

*I know that the healing
Of all our wounds
Is forgiveness
That permits a promise
Of our return
At the end.*[1]

It was hard for us, even though the doctor had been very patient, very gentle. We had waited long—finished school, found new work, settled down—and only then found we would have no children of our own; *could* have no children of our own. We spoke our disappointments, in the dark of the night, and then pulled away—each locking away sorrows where they might not be found, wishing to save each other's raw and tender spirit.

The decision to adopt was easy. Placing the order was less so. "Find us a baby," we said to them. "We want a baby exactly like one of our own. Exactly!" They thought not. Babies of Irish and Chinese descent are rare in New Mexico. Long months later, the phone rang. They called to tell us, incredulously, "We have your baby!" A new kind of joy came into our house. We called him "Pat."

Not many months passed, and with them, the joy. Pat was stricken with fever, seizures, brain damage. But prayers, love, and the warm grasp of God prevailed. Pat lived, and a special joy brightened our lives for almost eleven years. And then he was taken. That joy fled with him in a way as unexpected and abrupt as his arrival. Isaac Watts's old hymn played over and over in my head:

> Time, like an ever-rolling stream
> Bears all its sons away;
> They fly forgotten, as a dream
> Dies at the opening day.[2]

That occurred almost twenty years ago. It has been, for us, a long trek in the Valley of the Shadow. Friends told us at the time, "You'll get over it." One observed, "Not completely. A loss is always a loss." Geoffrey Spencer, a special friend and fellow sojourner, perceives a critical difference between grief and loss. Very often we grieve, he says, as the result of tragedy that occurs in the lives of others but impacts us personally. Loss is the experience of misfortunes occurring in our own experience.

Some of life's adventures combine both of these and more. Yes—we grieve because of the affliction, pain, and struggle that was Pat's lot. We sorrow for his brief, difficult span, And yes, again, we suffer loss as his absence is an emptiness in *our* days.

Years back, Peggy Lee made popular a particularly stirring song, "Is That All There Is?" A perceptive query, it may be one of the singular questions raised for people anywhere at any time. If the story of our years with Pat, as abridged above, were the whole story, the search for meaning and spiritual sustenance would be fruitless and to no avail whatsoever. We would remain in the Valley, closing our story with the words of Job:

A mortal, born of a woman,
Few of days and full of trouble,
Comes up like a flower and withers,
Flees like a shadow and does not last.
—Job 14:1–2

The psalmist, declaring his faith stance *vis-à-vis* the "Valley of the Shadow of Death," states that fear is vanquished because of the presence of the living God. Such a faith is a growing thing and depends a great deal on our gift for hindsight and reflection, which allows us to put our past experience in a particular perspective and arms us for what is yet to be. Looking back on our own experience of grief and loss, three lessons stand in bold relief, not fully appreciated at the time, but serving as present encouragement and strength.

First of all, the concern of our loving Father can prepare us for much of what befalls, if we are sensitive and concerned, and know in our hearts that "this" is not "all there us." The day before death of our son, my wife had an unusual experience in which she was told what she needed to know and shown all the things she would need to do as events unfolded. It is my conviction that, were she not a person who takes her "Sainthood" seriously, such preparation would not have been possible. She would have been unready and unable to receive it. What a blessing and source of joy to sense that, when the Valley opens before you, you know that you will not be alone and adrift.

Second, much power and most requisite support for our needs came through the love and inspired presence of others—brothers and sisters in this great aggregation of God's children. On the night of Pat's death, we drove home from the hospital, a journey of several hours. It was late when we pulled up in front of our house. There, standing in the street in nightgown and robe, was our beloved neighbor, Kay. She said, simply, that she couldn't stand to see us come home alone on such a night. The shadows in the Valley pale in the presence of people who incarnate the joy of love shared in care and concern. We call this deep personal connection *community*. This is a universal truth, manifest in the experience of all humankind. Consider the testimony of the first-century Chinese sage:

The dead are gone, and with them we cannot converse.
The living are here and ought to have our love.[3]

Third, the restoration of balance and wholeness, recovery from loss and healing of grief, depends to a great extent on our own determination to choose joy as our stance in this world of confusion. Key to this process (and it is a process, not an event) is our willingness to cull the depths for the lessons to be learned and the clues for what joy might be. Years before much of this came to pass, a friend and colleague, John Muceus, told me of an experience he had while driving across western Oklahoma. Responding to a strong urge to stop, he paused to write the thoughts that were impressed on his mind. Sometime later he shared this writing with me. I have it in my papers . It was addressed to me, personally. After being reminded of God's love for me, I was told that I would not enjoy the fellowship and joy that would be normal for a father and son. However, there would be those who would be as "spiritual sons" to me, and my relationship with them would be of such richness that I would not miss what I desired to share with Pat. This has come to pass.

Through the years, as we have lived in different locales, I have responded to deep feelings directing my attention to certain individuals for whom I have felt a strong stewardship of connection. These relationships have been sources of joy and fulfillment, and I have seen them as arising from sensitivities and needs resulting from these former experiences that, if not mined for significance, would leave me much the poorer.

I do not for a moment believe Pat suffered and died so we could experience blessings that otherwise would have been unavailable to us. That is a faulty and perverse theology. My conviction is that, as Lehi stated in the book of II Nephi, we are that we might have joy. That joy is always an option to us if we seriously seek sources of love, fellowship, growth, and service, even when faced with the awful possibilities life can hold—there, in the Valley.

Notes

1. Alice Walker, "Goodnight, Willie Lee, I'll See You in the Morning," in Mary Jane Moffatt, ed., *In the Midst of Winter* (New York: Vintage Books/Random House, 1982), 264.
2. Isaac Watts, "O God Our Help," in *Hymns of the Saints* (1981), #200.
3. Arthur Waley, trans., "Mei Sheng and Fu I," see Mary Jane Moffatt above.

Chapter 12

 **in Times of Grief**

When We Walk with a Limp
By Geoff Spencer

> *If life is to be meaningful and satisfying, we must attach ourselves deeply and fully to people and causes. Yet everything to which we do and can attach is finite.*[1]

On January 9, 1998, with the consent of his parents, the medical staff at Research Medical Center in Kansas City, Missouri, removed the life-maintenance equipment from our grandson Connor. Born three months premature, his prospects of survival had always been remote, and now, at the age of three weeks, all hope had gone. In company with Becky Shalley, an elder from the congregation, I had laid fingers on a head too small to accommodate our hands, and asked a blessing for him and his parents. Now we, as his grandparents and uncles on the scene, came together with Connor and his parents in a quiet room thoughtfully provided by the hospital, while his doctor came in periodically to check his all-too-weak "vital" signs, he gradually slipped away from us.

We had been prepared, virtually from the moment of his birth, for this harrowing experience, but again not prepared. How could we be prepared? There were things immediately to be done: a service of commemoration to be planned, visiting family to be accommodated, sympathetic friends to be welcomed, cards to be sent, and phone calls to be attended to. And then came the long, slow days and nights of quiet grief and emptiness in place of the anticipated sounds and activities of a new life.

At such times our lives may become more like a *wandering* rather than a *journey.* Yet we can only insulate ourselves from such times at the risk of becoming so unfeeling that nothing touches us outside our own egocentric selves. But if we live in caring relationships with others, there will inevitably be pain in loss. As difficult as it might be for us to believe at the outset, grief has a part in the recovery:

> **Suddenly we realize that we must travel into the future carrying not any past, but our particular past, a past that cannot be changed. Whatever freedom means, we are not free to undo this past. The freedom comes in how we relate this past to our future. We can drown ourselves in regret, lose ourselves in nostalgia, or cling to these old injuries and losses. But if we do, it is our *choice*, not our destiny.[2]**

I do not know how, and have not found any way to disown the pain, or deny it, and still remain in touch with reality. But just as grief may help us to preserve the meaningfulness of the past, it may serve as a midwife, if you will, in letting us recover the sense of journey. For even while we grieve there are things to be done, appointments to be kept, tasks to be completed, deadlines to be met, even perhaps other friends to comfort in their time of grief. As much as we might wish for it, there do not appear to be any "timeouts" in the ongoing journey of our lives. During such times, as John Raines has observed, "we may walk with a limp, so to speak. But we do walk." The very energy of limping, strange to us at first, and requiring its own kind of concentration, is part of the exercise of recovery and moving on, and discovering again the element of joy as a gift of grace.

In the depth of this experience, I encountered a dimension to grief that I should already have known. From a source that escapes me, I recall the words of another who mourned the loss of a loved one: *"I shall look at the world through tears. Perhaps I shall see things that dry-eyed I could not see."* How can it be that the experience of grief can give rise to an unusual sensitivity to the pain and suffering that exists all around us, so often hidden, it would seem, by the myopia so easily induced by the pleasure and enjoyment of the "good" life? Even while we walk with a limp, our vision, through tears, may open to us a source of strength and compassion that extends beyond our own awareness of pain.

If it is not too presumptuous to adapt a description applied to Isaiah's "suffering servant" (Isaiah 53:3) we are, each one of us, people "of sorrows and acquainted with grief." A longtime pastor and counselor, Wayne E. Oates, has described the many kinds of situations in which we suffer separation and pain.[3] Anticipatory grief is related to the gradual loss of life due to a terminal disease: sudden or traumatic grief comes with little or no warning: chronic or "no end" sorrow may arise from living with a deformed or retarded child, or a spouse suffering from Alzheimer's. There is the tragic sense of life embodied in the kind of grief "that arises from the sense of being limited in our care of others and the sense of being subject to death ourselves,"[4] described by the poet Wordsworth as "the still sad music of humanity." Wayne Oates writes with a view to offering help for counselors and pastors, but each one of us needs help in the very integral dimensions of life's journey, when we walk through "the valley of the shadow of death."

There are the less obvious, but nevertheless painful times of loss and separation encountered in childhood and adolescence, and then the griefs of adult life and older adulthood: death of a spouse, of a child or grandchild, spontaneous miscarriage, birth of a malformed child, divorce, work-related separation. For many RLDS members in recent years there has been the very real grief of separation from those who formerly shared the same faith journey. This will be true while ever we maintain what is most meaningful in life—deep attachments to people and causes in a world marked by finitude.

It will also be true that, in the midst of grief and separation, we do have a choice. As Tim Hansel reminds us:

> Pain is inevitable, but misery is optional. We cannot avoid pain, but we can avoid joy…. At any moment in life we have at least two options, and one of them is to choose an attitude of gratitude, a posture of grace, a commitment to joy.[5]

And so here, too, we can choose joy, not speedily or easily, but eventually, and by the sweet presence of that mysterious grace breaking in upon us from time to time, and often when we least expect it. Joy, consciously embraced, never leaves us where we were, but further along in the journey, and stronger because of it:

Growth requires the courage to be at each new era of life and the courage to take the leap of faith into each new era of life. As we look on separations that occur at each new era of the life cycle as calling for this kind of courage then the experience of dying from an old era and being born into a new existence brings with it both pain and joy, both a kind of death and a kind of resurrection. If we focus these experiences on the presence of the living Christ, we are never alone.[6]

Is this nothing more than "PR" for people who need a pep talk when in the "pits"? I think not, and my experience, along with what I have observed in the bewildering array of grief experiences in others, is that the "good tidings of great joy" that came with Jesus is still sufficient in every experience of life, though for a while we may walk with a limp. John Raines concludes his insightful editorial on grief thus:

Since we cannot wish one another a life without significant loss, let us wish for one another instead a strange gift—one that is recognized as a gift only in retrospect; let us wish for one another the gift of good grieving.[7]

One Person's Journey Through Grief
By Patti Kome

On January 25, 1997, Dale Kome, a member of the Chula Vista, California congregation was severely injured in an airplane crash. Two weeks later, on February 8, despite intensive efforts to treat the burns suffered in the accident, and other complications, Dale died. The Christmas letter for that year from his widow Patti, describes her journey of faith.

I do not desire to cause any sadness during a season of joy and celebration—yet, just as I am not trying to escape from my own grieving process, I know I cannot but be real with you—you who care about me and have shared with me over the loss of Dale this past year.

As you can probably imagine, this has been the saddest and most difficult year of my life in having to face and deal with Dale's death. The depth of pain and sorrow is unbelievable! I miss him in a thousand different ways for Dale was a remarkable man and a wonderful husband, father, grandfather, and my dearest friend.

Yet I have begun to work through my grief of such a profound loss (which at best I understand takes two to three years). I have experienced tremendous love and support from my family, friends, acquaintances, people I don't know, and most of all from my heavenly Father. The support has been overwhelming, and I am deeply grateful for the ongoing love and caring that I receive daily from so many of you. I cannot begin to tell you how much your expressions of love and your prayers have helped me and meant to me....

Even though there are still particular struggles and challenges I am having to deal with as a result of this accident... I feel overwhelmed with gratitude to my Lord for all of his blessings through this continuing ordeal. These give me courage to face the future trusting in my God who has promised me that "He will be with me every step of the way."...

I keep very busy taking care of everything at home (of course, everything has broken down it seems!) and I continue to play for all of the services at church and I attempt to participate and minister to others as I feel I am able. I just completed a ten-week class (one session a week) on grief which was very helpful and I plan to join a grief support group for widows after the first of the year.

In closing, I would like to say that I do not think Dale's accident and resulting death were "God's will." I believe that because God has granted us the freedom of choice, sometimes the choices we make or others make cause harm either to ourselves or someone else. God honors that freedom to choose and for the most part allows the natural consequences of our actions. I do not understand why God did not intercede or protect or heal Dale but this I do know: God has been with me and I have decided to trust him even though I do not understand. I know that is the only way to ever find peace and joy in my life again someday.

First Steps to Recovery
By Shawn Parton

At a memorial service held to celebrate the brief life of Connor, whose death was described at the beginning of this chapter, his father wrote, and his uncle Paul Spencer read the following letter. It reflects the first steps by the family to deal with their grief.

Dear Connor,

Three years ago your friends and family gathered in this special place for the blessing of your brother, Luke. On that occasion, Papa Geoff had your mother and me compose a letter to Luke. On that occasion I asked that Luke would have the wisdom to realize that every moment on this earth is precious and wonderful, and that our lives as humans are far too short and fragile to waste any time regretting the past, ignoring the present, and waiting for tomorrow. We don't know if Luke will have that wisdom, but I do know your mother does. I would like to think she got that way by listening to your dad, but I know better.

Connor, from the moment you joined us in the world, your mother did everything possible to ensure your short stay with us was the best it could be. Armed only with a cordless telephone and a four-color ballpoint pen, your mother coordinated three trips a day to the hospital and day-care for Luke. Your mother, with the help of your grandparents, uncles, and friends, made sure she saw you and shared herself with you as much as she possibly could. She did not let her lengthy stay in the hospital, or her surgery, slow her down at all. Within a week she was able to do many of the nursing procedures for you herself.

Connor, your brother Luke did as much as anyone could expect. When we took him to see you, he made sure everyone in the neonatal ICU knew we had all washed our hands and put "gown-shirts" on. Luke was always excited to go see you at the hospital. He was always cheerful while he looked at you, and now is sad because he can't go see his baby brother, Connor, anymore.

Your mother, father, and brother would have had a very difficult time without the support of many people. Your relatives have traveled many miles and made numerous trips to help us. They put aside their own needs to help us help you. Your Grandma and Grandpa Parton, Uncle Mark, Uncle Paul, and Meg, have yo-yoed back and forth across the country to do what they could for you and your parents. All of our friends, neighbors, employers, and co-workers have been nothing but generous, kind, and thoughtful in their endeavors to assist us. The staff at Research was also very special. All the people were great, and some were absolutely heroic in their care for you and your mother.

Connor, we hope that during your brief stay with us you felt the love we had for you and the love that everyone provided for us. Even though we lost you, your family has been blessed with a wonderful experience. All of us, especially your mother, fought the good fight to keep you with us in this world. It is with great sadness and disappointment we celebrate your life and say goodbye. Connor, please know that we did the best we could for you each and every day.

All our love,
Mom, Dad, and Luke

Notes

1. John C. Raines, "The Goodness of Grief," in *The Christian Century* (October 15, 1986): 886.
2. Ibid.
3. Wayne E. Oates, *Grief, Transition, and Loss* (Minneapolis, Minnesota: Fortress Press, 1997). The book is a practical guide for pastors, and part of the Creative Pastoral Care and Counseling Series.
4. Ibid., 25.
5. Tim Hansel, *You Gotta Keep Dancin'*, 55.
6. Wayne E. Oates, 86.
7. John C. Raines, "The Goodness of Grief," 887.

Chapter 13

 **in the Times of Loss**

Can't I Hold on Just a Little Longer?
By Geoff Spencer

*Losses are a part of life— universal, unavoidable, inexorable. And
these losses are necessary because we grow by losing and leaving,
and letting go.... For the road to human development is paved with
renunciation. Throughout our life we grow by giving up.[1]*

For more than twenty-five years I have been a serious reader of
English mystery stories. I have had my favorite authors and have
endeavored to read everything they wrote. Occasionally, over that
span of years, an author will die. When that happens, I feel I have
suffered a real loss and may even feel resentful because they have
left me to fill the gap caused by their passing.

For perhaps twice as long as that I have collected books: books
related to school programs in which I was enrolled, but books on
many other subjects as well: history (English, Australian, American), religion, poetry and music, sociology, travel, and such mun-
dane things as cricket and Australian novels. But it has become
obvious that I must put a stop to this particular form of consumer-
ism and indeed begin reducing the space taken up by my books.
And so I have been giving them away. But even to give away books
I have not yet—and probably never will—read is painful. Indeed,
if only I could recall an occasion when I have given away something that I really needed I might feel justified in my hurt. So far,
that has never happened.

Nevertheless, letting go is difficult. So many folders of notes I
have made during school programs over a period of thirty years—

out they go, consigned to oblivion. So many carefully filed articles from the *Herald* reaching back to the time when my parents bequeathed me their copies of the church magazine from the 1930s and onward. Summaries of workshops and seminars, boxes of filing cards of quotations; these too must be pruned. I know it needs to be done. I have derived a great deal of pleasure, and some advantage, from the experience of gathering. But it hurts.

These examples, trifling as they may be, nevertheless point to a pervasive dimension of our lives. From the time we move away from total dependence on mother, and then family, losing the innocence of childhood in the process, we may well be tempted to affirm the judgment pronounced by one eight-year-old philosopher: "losing sucks." In most cases, the frequency of losses increases during the second half of an average lifetime, until the final loss that is indeed universal and unavoidable. The phenomenon of loss prompted the celebrated columnist and author, Judith Viorst, to write the book titled *Necessary Losses: The Loves, Illusions, Dependencies and Impossible Expectations that All of Us Have to Give Up in Order to Grow*. It is an unpalatable thought, but Viorst states:

> **I would like to propose in this book that the people we are and the lives that we lead are determined, for better and worse, by our loss experiences.**[2]

Until not so long ago energy was something that I expended casually and without thought. I might become fatigued, but recovering was no major problem. Now I find myself, sometimes against my will, reviewing the day ahead, measuring what is projected against my energy bank, and deciding whether I can accomplish what I have planned to do, and what must regretfully be left to another day.

There is scarcely one dimension of life that escapes the experience of loss. The pleasant forms of childhood play and learning give way to the sterner disciplines of continuing education. The freedoms of single life are inevitably succeeded by the disciplines of marriage and parenthood. Tasks that might be performed almost without a thought to the energy needed become more burdensome, and many of them must be given up with the passage of time. Advancing years may be accompanied by loss of bodily functions—sight, hearing, mental awareness, agility, and endurance—not to mention teeth, hair, waist size.

It has long been recognized that retirement brings its particular challenges to adjustment, especially for those whose sense of worth, significant relationships, and opportunities for upward mobility have been work-related. In more recent times, however, the incidence of mergers, leveraged buyouts, and hostile take-overs has rendered the workplace uncertain even before retirement. The practice of "downsizing," a euphemistic term invented by those who manage the process to be applied to others, is an ever-present threat in the corporate world.

For many of us, the daily obituary column can be a constant reminder of what is happening to our contemporaries. We will never recognize the names of dear friends without the discomforting thought that the time will come when we will all "make the news," so to speak. In the meantime, we are obliged to confess, "Old age... is what you're stuck with if you want a long life."[3]

There are times when loss strikes us "out of season." Chronic or serious illness may bring with it disability and deprivation of expected freedom of movement. In our household we have learned to adjust to Parkinson's disease and the aftermath of four major surgeries, and yet there is little compensation or satisfaction in rehearsing the "if onlys." Not everybody thus afflicted can respond with the same courage and commitment to joy as did the two persons who share their testimony later in this chapter. It would be foolish to conclude that their positive adjustment was achieved once and for all, or without monumental struggle. But it would appear that they, and perhaps we under some of the many circumstances of loss or deprivation, have sensed the truth of the psalmist's claim: "Weeping may linger for the night, but joy comes with the morning" (Psalm 30:5 NRSV). The night may be long, but the morning does come, a gift of grace from God, an offering from loving friends, and a confirmation of the inner awareness that we were made for joy.

We can probably all remember, or are acquainted with, people who have not been able to make the adjustments demanded by the renunciations that were necessary in their lives: individuals who yearn for a youthful energy and achievement, who have never recovered from a longed-for relationship, who resent the loss of freedom required by parenthood, or mourn the loss of a position of prominence or who remain permanently crippled by the loss of a spouse. These are folk who have, consciously or otherwise, made the decision to "enjoy" misery and ignore joy; even though it will almost certainly be a shallow enjoyment.

The New Testament letter to the congregation in Philippi is unquestionably written by Paul, and while he was imprisoned. Nevertheless it carries an unmistakable note of confidence and joy. Whatever he had lost, he counted as nothing when weighed against the gain of finding Christ (see Philippians 3:7–8). The New English Bible's rendition of Paul's testimony could without doubt be replicated by many who have learned to live with loss:

I have learned to find resources in myself whatever my circumstances. I know what it is to be brought low, and I know what it is to have plenty. I have been very thoroughly initiated into the human lot with all its ups and downs—fullness and hunger, plenty and want. I have strength for anything through him who gives me power.—Philippians 4:12–13 NEB

So we learn to live with the letting go. From the first moment of birth, when we lose the intimate physical connection with a mother, to the moment when we draw our final breath, we live with the terminal disease called life, and celebrate the grace that sustains us though every moment of our existence.

Two Who Chose Joy
By *Maureen Harvey and Tukey Seagraves*

The testimonies of, Maureen Harvey of Detroit and Tukey Seagraves of San Francisco speak for themselves. Both describe a struggle with a potentially crippling disease, and the "baptism" in joy that ensued.

The Lord lifted me out of the muck and mire of self-hatred and low self-esteem, as well as from a depression that was ongoing and from which I never thought a cure was possible.

My miracle came through what I can only refer to as a blessing in disguise. In 1988 I was diagnosed with post polio syndrome (PPS) and told I would need to go back into a right-knee brace. This was devastating news for me. I then turned to the only one who could understand—my heavenly Father. One night I poured out my heart to him. I remember crying, not in anger but in self-pity and telling the Lord that I loved him, when out of my own mouth came the words, "Thank you." I found myself in total disbelief I could be giving thanks to God for post polio syndrome. Suddenly a peace came over me and an understanding that something was to come out of this experience for which I needed to thank God. During this time I had a premonition I would be going into a wheelchair. However, I was reassured by my specialist that this was unlikely, and I dismissed the idea.

In 1992 I was diagnosed with PPS from the neck down, and the following year I was told that I could work only two hours every other day. By 1994 it was necessary for me to wear two leg braces and use an electric wheelchair. Had it not been for my forewarning, the news would have been devastating.

It was a very difficult time. I know that had it not been for my dependence on God I might not be here today. I had been diagnosed in 1988 with long-term depression. However, I found that the more I became dependent on God the happier and more fulfilled my life became.

One major turning point came when I was told I had a rapidly progressive form of PPS. It occurred to me that I was headed for a convalescent home. Once again I turned to the Lord with the need to know: What good could I be if I could not take care of myself? I sensed the words "I have great works for you to do." It took a week before I could go back to God with the question, "What great works could I do?" Again the answer came: "A smile to those in need of one." That experience has sustained me and given me strength for the future.

In 1995 I started to regain my strength. I have now been told I am in remission. There are times when I long to have all my strength back. However, the lessons I have learned from the experience have been invaluable. I can say with certainty that I would not want to go back to 1988. I have something quite special and priceless—a wonderful relationship with my heavenly Father. The gift that arises from that relationship is a joy of life that I never thought possible. No matter what comes I know I will always be thankful.

Maureen Harvey

You have a choice.
You can select joy over despair, happiness over tears,
Action over apathy and growth over stagnation.
You can select you—and you can select life.[4]

It was in July 1988 that my husband Dave and I sat in the doctor's office and listened as he explained how all the tests I had been undergoing indicated that I had multiple sclerosis. I wasn't sure at that point what that would mean, but I was sure it wasn't good. From the time we left the doctor's office until hours after we arrived back home I was in tears. This just couldn't be happening to me—*not now*. The more I read about multiple sclerosis the more frightened I became. There were a lot of symptoms associated with MS, but for some reason my fear seemed to focus on the possibility of losing the use of my legs.

In the weeks that followed I spent a lot of time in tears, looking at where I had been and where I thought I was headed. My life had been one filled with blessings. I had a wonderful husband, two beautiful children, a spacious home, terrific friends, and an inner life that seemed to be growing by leaps and bounds. I was happy. I was excited by what might be waiting ahead of me. I had the breeze on my face as I flew through the sky with the wonder of a baby bird on its first flight, wondering where this new experience would lead me. "This couldn't be happening to me. Why would God teach me to fly and then clip my wings?" My fear was turning into anger. I really became caught up in the "what ifs" and the depression was hard not only on me but on my family.

It didn't happen at a certain moment, or place, but over time I began to see that the negativism I was allowing to control my life was not how I wanted to live the rest of my life. My life was still lived with meaning and purpose; I still had the love and support of a wonderful family and caring friends. I had always been a positive person—what was happening was blocking the light of that positiveness.

In Marriage Enrichment training we were taught that "Love is a decision." That was something I had struggled with until I had experienced it for myself. But I can remember one morning feeling hurt at the angry words exchanged with my husband, and all of a sudden it occurred to me to think about what was happening. I could either sit all day and brood over what was really a silly little argument and have a horrible day, or I could decide I was going to just love him in spite of it. I had a choice. I chose to love, and my heart and my day were both lightened.

I am sure that this was the basis of my being able to come to grips with the diagnosis of MS. I came to see that joy is also a decision. I could choose to be happy. But I found that deciding to be happy isn't a one-time event. I still have long periods of good times when I don't even have to think about the MS. But I also continue to have bad days when I have to choose several times in one day that I am not going to let the depression that comes so easily control my life.

One particular event stands out in my mind. I noticed my right leg would not lift off the floor. Two days later the left leg also became affected. My worst fears seemed to be coming to fruition. It was a hard few months. But with the help of my family, my friends, a very positive neurologist, and mega-doses of prednisone I regained the use of my legs. In fact, six months later my husband and I made a very strenuous hike to the top of Half Dome in Yosemite National Park. Many people had accomplished this feat, but to me there was an extra sense of accomplishment. I had not only overcome my worst fears of having MS but had experienced one of the highest points of my life sitting on top of that mountain and gazing down into the beautiful Yosemite Valley. Somehow, having MS made the feeling of reaching the top even greater and more powerful.

I just recently finished reading Viktor Frankel's book *Man's Search for Meaning*. This man endured years of unspeakable horror in Nazi death camps. He was an internationally renowned psychiatrist who came from a wealthy family. Through this atrocious experience he lost everything he held dear. But listen to his words:

> **The experience of camp life shows that man does have a choice of action…. Man can preserve a vestige of spiritual freedom, of independence of mind, even in such terrible conditions of psychic and physical stress…. Everything can be taken from a man but one thing: the last of the human freedoms—to choose one's attitude in any given set of circumstances, to choose one's own way.**[5]

I choose joy.

Tukey Seagraves

Notes

1. Judith Viorst, *Necessary Losses* (New York: Simon and Schuster, 1986), 16.
2. Ibid., 17.
3. Ibid., 285–286.
4. Leo Buscaglia, as found on his Web site.
5. Viktor E. Frankel, *Man's Search for Meaning* (New York: Washington Square Press, published by Pocket Books, a division of Simon & Schuster, 1984 edition).

Chapter 14

A Time for Personal Joy

We conclude this brief study with chapters describing particular activities that have been sources of joy for us. Joy comes to us in virtually endless forms, from cultivating a beautiful garden to maintaining a combustion engine in perfect running order, from visiting friends who need company to conducting a well-balanced choir. And in every case we may experience the profound presence of what has been described, from a most unexpected source, as "the ineffable, the all-satisfying completeness of joy."*

As you are encouraged to identify your gifts, we invite you to identify your joys. If you have no hesitation about defacing (decorating) this book, make a note of them here. If you do, then make a list of them to place where you will frequently be reminded of them:

_____

_____

_____

_____

_____

Give thanks for the ways joy enriches your life. Do not hesitate to tell others about them. As far as possible, use them to bring joy to others. And above all, remember the grace that makes a fullness of joy available to us: If you heed my commands, you will dwell in my love.... I have spoken thus to you so that my joy may be in you, and your joy complete.—John 15:11, NEB

---

*   Agatha Christie, in "The House of Dreams," from *The Harlequin Tea Set* (New York: Berkley Books, 1998), 66.

Chapter 15

The  of Reading

By Frank Kelley

The old sedan was bestrewn with stickers, slogans, and proclamations; poetic, political, and prosaic. One stood out: "If You Can Read This, Thank a Teacher!" I could read it. So whom should I thank? Or rather, where shall I begin my thanking.

I cannot remember a time when I could not/did not read. I grew up blessed by parents who loved to own and read books, and who urged me to do likewise. Our community was graced by the presence of a genuine, complete library just for children. A local benefactor had bequeathed a mansion and fortune to establish such. I was rescued from the damp torpor of more endless Topeka summers than I can count by long walks to and from the cool stacks of the Mulvane followed by hours on the front porch with *Idylls of the King, Gods and Heroes*, and my first favorite author of fiction—Stephen W. Meader.

Weekend afternoons were often spent among the dark and musty stacks of the used-book store on Lower Kansas Avenue, the proprietor of which knew us by name. It was there, rummaging though unsorted stock, that we heard a scratchy music broadcast interrupted by the fateful news from Pearl Harbor.

On the grounds of the state capitol was the public library. It was drenched in a hush such as I never experienced at our little RLDS congregation. I sensed in the spirit of the place that it was a temple of sorts. Upstairs was the *sanctum sanctorum*, a shadowed reading room, dominated by palpable silence, enormous desks, lamps with green shades, and quiet, parchment-faced old men who, Mother assured me, were really very much alive.

It was in that same library, I learned later, that that same mother had broken the laws of the Lord and the land. Decades later, she gave me her copy of *Biographical Sketches of Joseph Smith the Prophet and His Progenitors for Many Generations* by Lucy Mack Smith. Handling the fragile, leather-bound volume (1880) carefully, I noted with great interest that the title page was embossed with the inscription, "Public Library—Topeka, Kansas."

Mother brushed off my interrogations. "They didn't even know they had that book! No one had checked it out for years and I thought it should be put to good use." I treasure that little volume. Someday I may return it to its shelves of origin, of course.

My father was self-educated, well read, and the product of a tiny community in far eastern Oklahoma, where he was schooled as far as the eighth grade. It was a major accomplishment then and there. He must receive the greatest measure of thanks for assisting me to read the bumper stickers of life.

Working on the railroad, in a country junction station where he tended manual switches and operated a telegraph key to direct train crews, he had blocks of quiet time interrupted by flurries of noise and action. He read. He made me read. A preschooler, I was set up on his desk and coaxed through reading aloud from the latest edition of the *Saints' Herald*, the local newspaper, and whatever else caught his fancy. It was a kind of mental inquisition, and today I could have had him charged with child abuse. But I learned to read.

Later, Dad encouraged me to keep a notebook listing books read, with dates and comments. If I were to fault this immersion in the printed page at such an early age, it would be for two lessons that took me well into middle age to unlearn: (1) a book must be read from cover to cover, front to back, in its entirety, and (2) one never marks in a book. I still bear the cerebral scars of such an approach to pedagogy, and lay aside an unfinished volume, or underline a special passage, with misgiving and traces of shame and guilt.

I can't imagine life without reading. It would be akin to solitary confinement, and the effects crippling, most likely in the way Leonardo Da Vinci described:

Iron rusts from disuse, stagnant water loses its purity, and in cold weather becomes frozen: even so does inaction sap the vigors of the mind.—From *Notebooks* (ca. 1500)

Often, riding the train into San Francisco, rather than basking in surroundings of green hills, blue water, and a startling skyline, I squint at the advertisements and instructions adorning the interior of the car. At the table, I study labels on the jars or the contents of the boxes of cereal or cartons of ice cream (what is guar gum?). I have even overturned chinaware to read the maker's trademark and name.

New books are nice, but used are better. To open a newly printed, pristine volume is much like donning a new shirt fresh from the store, stiff with sizing and smelling of chemicals and manufacture. It may be attractive, but it is without a history of its own. In Tahiti, I purchased books imported from France, printed and bound with page edges folded one to another. One had to sit with a blade and separate them before reading was possible. A Gallic friend said this was a rite to be savored, making the book uniquely one's very own. But I prefer books read, handled, and showing marks of use like Lucy Mack's biography of Joseph—perhaps my preference for veteran volumes is an inherited trait.

Used books present one with a life and history. They are best stalked in used-book stores, which offer stacks and jumbled piles in promising disarray. They exhibit a special patina detectable to the spirit as well as the eye.

I find some fiction is fine, but my reading needs a balance, a mental diet seasoned with reality, and blessed with generous helpings of great poetry. Such fare provides one with a healthy mix of intellectual and spiritual nourishment beyond that found in train cars, on jam labels, and the ubiquitous "Nutrition Facts" that grace every packaged comestible—except, thus far, the Communion emblems.

Thanks be to God, parents, and other special teachers along life's way. If there is a heaven, a glory celestial, it will have a plenitude of bookstores—used and new—that play good music, serve real ice cream, and pour rich cappuccino. I am excited by such eschatological possibilities. Are we not promised, at the last great day, we shall stand before God and the *books* will be opened? What a finish!

Chapter 16

The  of Singing

By Geoff Spencer

One day, when fell the Spirit's whisper, It touched to zeal the waiting throng; Inspiring hope and courage giving, To cultivate the gift of song.[1]

All human speech is a song, even though our normal oral speech mode may not utilize the full vocal range the voice is capable of producing. This would be noticeably true of some, like my fellow Australians, who are often accused of lacking color in speech. We may not display the cadences, the marvelous resolutions of hues and colors exhibited in singing. Nevertheless, in whatever mode of utterance we give voice to, we are never very far from singing.

I believe that human nature is adapted to singing, that there are certain moods, textures, intensities in human experience that are ultimately best expressed in singing. I am inclined to think it has always been this way; as long as there have been human beings conveying the emotions that distinguished their humanness—who had hopes, dreams, sorrows, achievements, despair, joy—just so long were there people who sang.

Perhaps such people, virtually inarticulate, when confronted with some majestic panorama, or beat upon by nature in its destructiveness, expressed their feelings of wonder and awe in singing. But they also sang as they began to be aware of some source of wonderment and otherness in the universe. Singing was the vehicle by which they gave voice to the conviction that their lives were not ultimately their own, but rested in some source of power beyond immediate experience and comprehension.

They sang in supplication, in thanksgiving, in praise—and when they did that they were singing our first hymns. And so we have done ever since, in every conceivable situation and condition. When I sing, I experience again the moods, hopes, and dreams of those who have bequeathed to us their lyrics. I understand that others may not respond in the same way, but this is the place for me to share my particular experience and testimony.

I have long appreciated the power with which one World War I poet lifted up the magic of singing to transcend even the most horrifying experiences of life. A wounded survivor of the monstrous insanity of that conflict, Siegfried Sassoon could still remember a situation when:

> **Everyone's voice was suddenly lifted,**
> **And beauty came like the setting sun,**
> **My heart was shaken with tears, and horror**
> **Drifted away... O, but everyone**
> **Was a bird, and the song was wordless; the**
> **Singing will never be done.**[2]

It gratifies me to know that the singing will indeed never be done. There are yet songs to be written, songs and songwriters who are as yet unknown to us. We share in a timeless process that has the power to transcend differences of culture and circumstance. Moreover, I believe that new songs often signify and herald the first wave of new ideas and enlightened understandings. Such ideas may be in the minds of theologians, reformers, or prophets, but they will most widely be communicated when shaped by the poets and embodied in the new songs that emerge for a new day. Not only is this true of the hymns that will find their way into our hymnals, but also in the "folk" songs that have so often focused the rallying point for a new awareness of human possibilities.

I am aware of the downside to the power of singing. Songs have inspired people to noble and laudable ends. But they have often given legitimacy to attitudes and acts of prejudice, barbarism, and destruction. There are few nations indeed whose gallery of songs does not include concepts to glorify war, racial superiority, or questionable values. As a growing boy I sang with wholehearted fervor the colonial and expansionist ambitions of the British Empire, even as it was on the path to extinction. Ironically, I am reminded of these words every time I hear the traditional graduation music for U.S. schools and colleges, from the first of Elgar's "Pomp and Circumstance" marches, to which we sang:

Land of hope and glory, mother of the free;
How shall we adore thee, who art born of thee.
Wider still and wider, shall the bounds be set;
God who made thee mighty, make thee mightier yet.
God, who made thee mighty, make thee mightier yet.[3]

The same temptation might surface in hymns that become popular, even loved by the Saints. I appreciated the provision laid down by Harold Neal when, as chair of the committee preparing *Hymns of the Saints,* (published by Herald House in 1981) he specified that every text, old or new, should be carefully reviewed before its acceptance and matching with a tune. This was to ensure that no words of dubious value should win acceptance on the basis of a popular or appealing tune. I had come to recognize that on several occasions I had mourned the loss of an old favorite on grounds of personal and nostalgic appeal rather than on the substance of the theology embedded in the text.

The hymn "What a Glorious Thing to Be in the Light" had already been moved to the "historical" section (whatever that was intended to mean) of *The Hymnal* (1956), though some people were not comforted by the apparent rejection of a well-loved hymn. Yet it was clear that to sing "Long the earth in darkness lay, without light" was to make a sweeping and most certainly presumptuous judgment about a major portion of Christian history from the restricted view of our RLDS tradition.

Nevertheless, even granting the need for caution, the singing will never be done. There will always be horrors to confront, barriers to be transcended, truth to be proclaimed, sin to be confessed, mystery to be acknowledged, and God to be praised.

In the peculiar workings of my mind, I imagine that ultimately there is just *one* hymn. There may be countless variations, but every one is a preface, a hint, a foretaste, if you will, of that ultimate hymn. Every other hymn, I am driven to believe, or more accurately, to *feel*, is in a sense unfinished. I think of the device of the unresolved chord, that leaves us with the conviction that something more needs to be added to bring a harmonious and satisfying conclusion. In this sense, every hymn is a *penultimate* hymn— an unresolved chord. Perhaps the best way to convey this impression is to cite the vision of John, recorded in the book of Revelation. It is not unlikely that such an ultimate event shall be accompanied by singing, and the agony and struggle of all human history shall be resolved in that ultimate hymn:

> **And I saw a new heaven and a new earth;**
> **For the first heaven and the first earth were passed away....**
> **And I saw the holy city, new Jerusalem,**
> **Coming down from God out of heaven....**
> **And I heard a great voice out of heaven saying,**
> **Behold, the tabernacle of God is with us,**
> **And God will dwell with us, and we shall be God's people.**
> **—Revelation 21:1–3**

And now a word of personal testimony. I have always loved singing, though at best a modest practitioner of the art. It was a joy to sing in the chapel of the Methodist school I attended as a high school student. Very early I became familiar with the hymns of the church in the small congregation in which I grew up. While a member of this congregation I sang in the choir of another, and when I was later assigned to teach in rural high schools as a teacher, I sang with Methodists, Anglicans, and Presbyterians. Later, on long car trips as an appointee minister, I would pass the time singing with the tape-recorded music—everything from Gilbert and Sullivan to the folk music of the 1960s and 1970s. But my most treasured experience was to sing in the congregations of the Saints, wherever I might be, even if I did not understand the language in which the text was rendered.

I can no longer do that to my satisfaction. My singing voice is now an embarrassment to me, and, I suspect, to others within hearing range. Advancing age and repeated surgeries have had their effect. While I mourn the loss of my ability to sing, I find myself appreciating the voices around me of those who must sing, as it were, on my behalf. And so I am able to find continuing joy in the assurance that, in one way or another, the singing will never be done.

Notes

1. Vida E. Smith, 1865–1945, Alt.
2. Siegfried Sassoon (1886–1967), "Everybody Sang."
3. "Land of Hope and Glory," a traditional British Empire patriotic song.

Joy of Notes

Joy of Notes

Joy of Notes

Choose Joy

By Francis W. Kelley and Geoffrey F. Spencer
With Supporting Testimonies

Joy is a word used a great deal in society today, and Christians in particular should be familiar with its meaning. Sadly, many people simply equate it with happiness, but there is so much more to joy than that. Even more distressing is the long history of Christianity that all too often presented a sober, serious, and humorless gospel—in short, an image of the "good news of Jesus Christ" as anything but joyful. Yet how can this be?

In *Choose Joy* two veteran appointee ministers in the Reorganized Church of Jesus Christ of Latter Day Saints, Frank Kelley and Geoff Spencer, offer their own perspectives on this essential attribute of the Christian life. Along with supporting testimonies from numerous others, they describe some of the circumstances and conditions in which we might experience the "joy of the gospel."

Some of these circumstances are not happy or pleasurable, of course. Yet the authors' basic thesis is that joy is an orientation, an attitude, that illuminates and undergirds all the varied experiences of life. It can transcend, reshape, and eventually transform even the most grievous or threatening event. After all, scripture records that human beings "are that they might have joy."

Each of the sixteen chapters in *Choose Joy* looks at a different aspect of joy in hopes that readers will reflect on their lives and, in turn, share joy widely with others. This book is ideal for use in organized class sessions, such as Sunday school, as well as for individual study and meditation.

ISBN 083090940-0

9 780830 909407

Printed in the USA